THE HUMAN DIMENSION

The Human Dimension

Coaching Adolescents and Young Adults

PAUL E. FINN, PhD

LUMINARE PRESS
WWW.LUMINAREPRESS.COM

To my wife: Jeanne Finn—
Very happy you said yes to this journey
together 47 years ago—
and it continues

CONTENTS

Introduction: Foundations 1

■ ONE
On Being a Coach 5

■ TWO
The Adolescent's Brain 16

■ THREE
Self-Fulfilling Prophecy and the
Two Faces of Mindfulness 36

■ FOUR
Coach as Teacher and Student 55

■ FIVE
Communication, Coach and Parent 71

■ SIX
Athlete/Coach Communication
and Goal Setting 84

■ SEVEN
Personality and Abnormal Psychology 111

■ EIGHT
Gender and Culture 126

■ NINE
Motivation, Performance, and
Sport Interventions 143

■ TEN
Getting into College 162

■ ELEVEN
Reflections From Senior Coaches 173

INTRODUCTION:
Foundations

Through both victory and defeat, as coaches we have a powerful effect on the development of the adolescent athlete. More than 90% of our adolescents will never see competition at a top tier DI University, experience a professional sports career, or play in the Olympics. Yet, on our fields they will learn humility in victory and character in defeat, and in supporting them through these lessons we are incredibly important mentors and teachers. Being a guide, with the requisite knowledge, is one of the great joys not just of coaching, but of life. Being a good guide is fundamental to our athletes' consistently winning in their sport and it is what serves as the foundation for each of the chapters ahead.

What is it about my own journey that has inspired me to want to share my experiences and accumulated knowledge with others? As a guide I have been informed by three areas of expertise: as a licensed psychologist, as a professor who has taught and advised over a thousand students over 35 years and conducted active published research, and as what hundreds of student athletes over the years have called me: Coach. I have somehow migrated past the typical retirement age, but because I still find great joy in all my work, I continue along the journey. My unusual combination of experiences provides me, I hope, with a seasoned orientation to coaching that can serve as a guide to others, no matter at what stage of the journey they find themselves.

As a psychologist, during my early years I worked with alcohol addiction through the National Institute of Alcohol Abuse and Addiction funded studies and internship. I have tested gifted children for placement recommendations and have been involved in Individualized Educational Plans (IEP) for children with challenges. With my doctoral degree I have both a counseling and clinical background with specific expertise in Health Psychology and have worked with folks with chronic pain, kidney disease, cardiac concerns and cancer as part of treatment teams.

I have interned and received considerable supervision in neuropsychology. I have conducted research and neuropsychological assessments. In addition to hospital work I have had a private practice and worked with a range of clients including athletes challenged with anxiety, depression and eating concerns. I evaluated concussions long before it was recognized publicly as a concern among athletics. This history has inevitably influenced my coaching philosophy and the approach I have taken towards athletes.

As a professor, I have guided many students on their academic journeys. My teaching and supervision have ranged from teaching 18 year olds General Psychology to supervising doctoral students in their pre-licensure postdoctoral year. I have helped guide many students towards a love of inquiry through research methods and writing, yielding presentations at conferences and published research. My students have received grant money for their research and presented results at professional conferences.

I have developed and taught new courses ranging from Psychology of Addiction to Exercise and Sport Psychology. I have been recognized by the American Psychological Association's honor society, Psi Chi, as national Faculty Advisor of the year; received our college's AAUP annual excellence in Faculty Accomplishment Award; and was named 'Honorary Senator' at Aurel Vlaicu University in Arad Romania.

As a coach I have coached college Division II varsity cross country (both men's and women's teams) for 15 years and have been responsible for everything from recruiting to remaining connected with the athletes after they graduate. Also, as my college did not have a varsity track program, I coached club track and field for 15 years, and have coached hundreds of young people to completing their first marathon.

Additionally, during my tenure as varsity coach I sponsored and ran summer cross country camps for area junior high schools and high school students. In these camps we used our college athletes to teach and train youth. I am Level I and Level II US Track and Field (USATF). As a coach I have attended annual national and regional coach conferences.

My greatest qualification for the advice I offer in the pages ahead comes from the many athletic and life journeys I have run and walked and hobbled with remarkable young athletes, students and clients. Most examples, not all, are slightly modified to respect identity of the athletes. Calling upon the many varied experiences I have had along the way as coach and integrating these with my experiences as a psychologist, teacher and researcher, I have undertaken the writing of this book. My hope in doing so is to encourage other coaches, whether new to the work or well-seasoned, and to provoke thought and opportunity for all of us to perhaps try new approaches to our sport.

In addition to my own clinical background and experiences, I offer valued expertise and resources provided by noted clinicians and researchers. I provide specific tips and strategies for coaching adolescents, none of which are limited to a specific sport, but are relevant to any adolescent who seeks your guidance in their development. Research and theories covered are translated from their psychological roots (for example, psychodynamic underpinnings) to sports applications without necessarily incorporating their roots.

Everything about my experiences and research has convinced me that coaching is ultimately about helping to guide the journeys of the cognitive, behavioral, social and overall physical development of our youth while simultaneously enjoying the exhilarating challenges of competition. To understand everything there is to know about our chosen sport is one thing, and it is necessary but not sufficient for the consistent win. To understand the sport and the athlete is foundational to winning as a team. I have also come to understand and appreciate that, whether we know it or not, our personal example as a coach ultimately influences the continued spiritual development of those we lead. What we do and how we do it has consequences that endure throughout the lifetimes of those who have called us coach. The goal of the chapters ahead is to offer you some concepts and tools based on my integrated and varied lifetime experiences as coach, psychologist and professor.

I write this book for all my XC, track and field and marathon athletes. More importantly I write this book for athletes yet to seek a coach. If I can offer one thing to you in the pages ahead it is this: we coach both the sport and the developing adolescent athlete. And if we do it well, with a care to the kind of enormous development taking place in the lives of individual athletes, our coaching will have value beyond any measure.

ONE

ON BEING A COACH

S tanding by Sean's hospice bed alongside his former teammates, I was struck by the sparkle in his eyes. ALS was taking his life all too soon. He had refused tube feeding and while embracing life, he had elected no extraordinary means to remain alive.

This was the Saturday of our annual home meet and the alum athletes had gathered today to cheer on their alma mater and to visit with their teammate, Sean. It was mid-afternoon by the time the meet had finished and we were driving as a group to the hospice facility. As we entered Sean's room, the joy on his face in seeing his fellow teammates was indescribable. Their expression of joy in seeing Sean was also evident, though mixed with heartache springing from their palpable sense of a vibrant life cut way too short.

It is impossible to measure the lasting impact of Sean's life and early passing. But its impact was certainly felt on both teams. Today, as I write this, an alum, announced her fundraiser in memory of Sean. Captain of the women's team when Sean was a competitive runner, she lives in Colorado, coaching high school cross country and track and field while in the winter she instructs skiers. She left a Boston-based cubicle as a researcher to explore the freedom and joy of the mountains of Colorado.

Here is a partial copy of her posting on Facebook "...
Before his passing, I told [Sean] of my plans to run a 100
miler [as a fundraiser for ALS]. This September 21st, I
hope to run the...Sangre de Cristo 100..." I have no doubt
she will complete the Sangre de Cristo 100-mile ultra-
marathon. She has the tools, physiological preparation and
discipline. And because of Sean she has all the motivation
she needs.

These are just two of the hundreds of people I have
coached over many years. Each and every one of them—as
athletes, as students, as people—has left me with warm
memories of their struggles in their growth and development. Of the many memories I cherish as a coach, most of
them are of the athletes and the team, not the final score.
Like most coaches I know, I have given 100% to place
individuals and teams in the best position to win their
meet or event or game. But long after any ribbons, medals,
or trophies have been distributed and found their place of
honor on shelves and walls, it is the lives of these athletes, in
whose journeys I have been humbled to share, that remain
indelibly with me.

Coaching the young ought to be a very rewarding
human experience both for the adolescent and the coach.
And as noted in the preface those rewards can extend a
lifetime for both the athlete and the coach. But as athletes
age and move beyond their participation in formal athletics,
what is it they remember? In my experience of coaching
in a college program, when athletes gather at their class
reunions, they rarely speak of their personal accomplishments. More frequently, their memories are of their team's
successes and, surprisingly, even its failings. What seems
more important to them are the close relationships they

developed as team members, the team cohesion, and the experience of being part of something larger than themselves. To understand this in coaching adolescents is central to successful coaching.

Coaches all want athletes to win, so we work hard with strategy, tactics, reviews of competition and specific skill development. A good coach knows that when the athlete follows their coach's program and wins, the win belongs to the athlete; but when the athlete is faithful to the coach's program and loses, it is the coach who loses the game or meet.

And yet coaching is so much more than the sport. Coaches serve as role models for humility in victory and development of character through defeat. As such, we are best described as *guides* for the development of our young men and women.

This guidance is a skill developed over time, just as teachers are guides in cognitive development. As a psychologist, I know that more than once it was the sport and the coach who kept a struggling student from dropping out of school. Indeed, I have on occasion included the need for continuation in sports as part of a student's Individualized Educational Plan (IEP).

Therefore, while many call you coach, as well they should, from my perspective it is best not to view yourself as a coach but rather as a guide. A guide is one who directs another on their journey. Don't get me wrong, I very much value the title of "coach." Yet I believe we need to rethink the incredibly difficult challenge of being a "coach" to the young. And here, as throughout this entire book, I use the term "coach" as synonymous with "guide."

Consider the way many persons first enter coaching the adolescent in junior high, high school or perhaps a town league. It is not unusual for a parent to find that, for any number of reasons, his or her child's team has suddenly been left without a coach. If this was your experience, and your entry into coaching began by being "voluntold," I am certain you can remember both the sense of loss of your team's previous coach and your own extreme apprehension in facing your new and daunting task. This task is one of learning the details of the game, the fear of a beloved neighbor asking why their lovely child did not get much playing time, or the friend who looks at you like you don't know how to enter a substitute into the game or how to rally a defense.

Perhaps your entry into coaching was as a young college graduate entering your first teaching job at a local high school. Being told you have been hired as a new English teacher was indeed exciting for you. But then, along with the conversation about being a new hire came the additional surprise assignment that you would need to coach a team in your new school—whether you have ever coached in the past or not. Depending on your background this new assignment can seem both exciting and daunting.

First time coaches commonly seek advice from a wise elder or contact a college friend who may have played the sport. It can be hard to seek advice from an elder as that is an admission of ignorance, which, for new faculty, is indeed a difficult admission. But having a sage mentor is as important in coaching as it is in education or even life.

Beyond a mentor or college friend, there are other resources for you. Many accessible books and volumes of YouTube videos are available for any sport, ranging from strategies to field tactics to conditioning and such. While it is initially difficult to know which readings or videos are of value to you, you proceed with the caution of a new coach.

Perhaps you played a sport in college. This would seem to make life easy or easier than if you had not played. You know the rules and basic game strategy, but you also are limited in knowing them from the perspective of *your* coach and what worked for *you* with *your* physical talent and personality. To apply your lessons to all young athletes, however, can be a mistake. Also, as you engage the learning process, it becomes especially challenging if, for example, your college sport was quite different from the sport you are being asked to coach. You may be asked to coach more of a ballistics skill like coaching the defensive line of a football team where the athlete requires explosive strength, and you are entering with the history of an endurance athlete.

This new challenge is made more daunting by the fact that you know you will soon be evaluated by parents and fans at a game or meet. All of your successes and failures will be public ones. Unlike the classroom, your every decision will be open and available to appraisal by a wide audience of subjective observers who will scrutinize game plays, position assignments, what members of the team play and who sits, conditioning, broad strategies and specific tactics. Then of course coaching adolescents who may be in junior high or high school carries with it its own set of developmental challenges. Add to all this the challenges that accompany leading a team whose members differ across age, gender, race, culture, religion, physical talent and so on.

Faced with all of these challenges of succeeding as a new coach in this new sport, it is easy to overlook your primary responsibility. That is, the responsibility of being a guide to young people in their development. As a teacher, you know development of the individual is primary; as a coach, this is often lost to the challenge of the win.

To sacrifice oneself, to practice when no one is watching, to console a fellow team member who lost the game you knew you could have won, to sit when you want to play are social, emotional and cognitive learning opportunities which are of great value in the adolescent's development. When you help a young person approach winning with humility and losing with dignity as well as learn to sacrifice their self for the team, you are helping to lay a great foundation for developing a valued member of the adult community.

The coach who understands this and is equipped to respond is *truly* a teacher, mentor and guide whose value is great. Also, this is a coach who, when combining this understanding with knowledge of the sport, is likely to win many games or meets.

Indeed we all love the proverbial thrill of victory. However we need to carefully decide what it means to win. We need to bring winning or losing into a larger perspective addressing the developing adolescent athlete. To be that coach who watches the team make the critical game score is truly exciting. On the other hand, as I said above, to be the coach who recognizes they own the game loss because of a strategic coaching error can lead a good coach to silent dejection. Even if all members execute their task well and are conditioned and ready, the scoreboard still truly does not 'tell it all.'

As you studied to become a teacher and took your practicum classes and completed your papers, you learned many of the fundamental skills of being a teacher. You learned that your job was more than guiding a young person in reading, writing and arithmetic. You learned that you would guide them in developing a thirst for knowledge, a drive toward the ability to think critically and reason which would continue to develop along their life journey—long after their guide is gone.

Many of the skills you learned as a guide in education are similar to those of a coach. As a coach—be it as a teacher, parent, neighbor or full time coach—you bring forward your unique personality, character traits, motivations, good and bad habits and quirks. While we are all just a bit different in how we apply our personalities to our tasks, there are fundamental qualities of a good teacher that parallel the good coach. Here is one example of a list of those qualities that make a great teacher:

- expert communication skills

- superior listening skills

- deep knowledge and passion for their subject matter

- the ability to build caring relationships with students

- friendliness and approachability

- excellent preparation and organization skills

- strong work ethic

- community-building skills

- high expectations for all[1]

As you review these qualities and as you work hard to develop these qualities you should know that whether guiding as teacher, parent or coach, the qualities are the same.

---

1. (https://owlcation.com/academia/Characteristics-Of-A-Good-Teacher)

Over the years I have had the pleasure of attending many national coaching conferences. I have sought and taken the opportunity to have lunch or dinner with Hall of Fame coaches. An example of a Hall of Fame Coach can be a track coach who has won national college/university championships and, in addition, that person may have also succeeded in having coached individual national All Stars and perhaps an Olympic contender. In other words, nationally recognized Hall of Fame Coaches are among the best of the best in their sport.

As you might expect, 'Hall of Fame' coaches are fascinating individuals. While they all love to compete and win, their personalities are quite varied. Still, I have observed from my time with them some consistent patterns of attitudes and behavior.

First, the Hall of Fame coaches I have met at these national meetings tend to be quiet listeners to others at the table. They are not out blustering about their wins or memories of specific great game plays. Rather, they seem to enjoy listening to others. Indeed, I found it necessary to encourage them to speak of their interests and histories in their sport even while former athletes who are now coaches themselves were interrupting our conversation to smile, shake hands and share greetings. You see, even as I was trying to make it about them, it was about others.

At one luncheon a former athlete said to his coach, "Come on, coach, show us your ring." It was a ring the coach had received after his team won the national championship. The coach hesitated and with a note of mild embarrassment said, "I don't carry it, my wife has it." She was sitting next to him. With what I interpreted as a look of pride in her husband, she produced the ring to the joy of his athletes.

The coach not only clearly expressed humility in relating his success, the reward for his success was something a loved one carried for him.

The second characteristic I note about many Hall of Fame coaches is they are very interested in learning as much as possible. They are seeking an advantage with knowledge and are confident that they could be smarter than they are—even though they are Hall of Fame coaches! Also, they do not seem embarrassed to seek to learn. Indeed they are among some of the most knowledgeable people I have met and they continue to ask questions. Further, they don't respond to popular trends, or what specific strategy a team used to win in a particular year (though they appreciate knowing this). Rather, they seek the underlying theory and science that lies behind the curtain of public appeal and popular magazines. This hunger to be a little bit better and a little bit smarter reveals itself consistently across these Hall of Fame coaches.

Third, Hall of Fame coaches truly believe the devil, as well as the best opportunity for success, lies in the details. They know that producing a star athlete requires them to know the physical, emotional, cognitive and relational characteristics of the athlete. Next, they build an annual training program fitting both the rigors of science and the uniqueness of that athlete. For example, a high school football coach may know how to set up an annual program for developing a talented football player, but likewise appreciates how this particular athlete also loves playing lacrosse, therefore molding a program which includes the opportunity to both play lacrosse and benefit from the training lacrosse offers the athlete.

Also, for example, the coach who seeks detailed knowledge appreciates that while many coaches may speak of lactate (produced from hard aerobic/anaerobic exertion) as negative and unproductive, at certain levels of exertion, the body consumes and benefits from lactate. This has incredible implications for the science of coaching when it comes to training schedules in preseason and getting ready for "the big competition." The coach who knows the science as well as the art of the game and the athlete often makes coaching look easy to the casual observer.

One additional point here: well over 90% of our adolescents who play sports are not destined for the Olympics or for fully funded DI scholarships. To make our adolescent athletes believe in themselves is important, but, with few exceptions, to treat our adolescents with the rigor of Olympic expectations is unfair. By this I mean the 14 year-old who wants to be a dual sport athlete should be encouraged to explore their options, and as coaches we can adapt and modify schedules to optimize their experiences. We need to balance high expectations with pragmatics in the adolescent's development. The multi-sport athlete is far less common today than in the past and that is indeed unfortunate. It is unfortunate as playing more than one sport assists in developing different physical aspects of the young athlete. Also, the athlete is exposed to different coaches, philosophies and team members. Together these provide unique learning experiences not available to the single sport athlete.

Perhaps surprisingly, a fourth trait of Hall of Fame coaches is love. While they have dramatically different personalities, every one of them demonstrates a fundamental love for their athletes. One coach may be seen as gruff.

Another may frequently raise her voice, and yet the athlete quietly admits, "It's okay as coach really cares for us."

As a teacher, when a student fails an exam it is common for them to leave the room to talk with friends and text parents. The teacher does not typically see the defeat the student experiences. But the athlete's defeat is usually directly experienced by the coach and often sends the coach back to his or her desk late at night to review all aspects of training to best help the athlete improve. Unlike coaches, teachers typically don't ride home on a bus with a student after the student experiences a failure. Also a teacher seldom has to reflect on how a student's failure will affect the future performance of other students in the class.

This challenge is even greater when the coach of a city league is the parent of a player. Now the coach rides home with at least one athlete and must reconcile parent with coach. This challenge is discussed in Chapter 5.

Surely there are other qualities and characteristics of Hall of Fame coaches, but these four are the ones that stand out from my years of observation and conversations. Knowing one's sport extremely well is a given. But to be a good listener, a seeker of practical and theoretical knowledge, to be attentive to the details of the science and art of one's sport, and to care deeply about the athletes in your charge—these traits represent the best of the guides in our society, be they coaches, teachers, physicians, therapists, political leaders or CEOs.

TWO

THE ADOLESCENT'S BRAIN

The human brain continues to develop throughout adolescence and as the adolescent continues to learn, the pre-frontal lobes grow in size. This part of the brain, as has now been explained in many books, is responsible for, among other things, decision-making, planning, judging, maintaining attention and inhibition of impulses that may or may not be societally acceptable. In other words, the pre-frontal region is the Chief Executive Officer (CEO) of our brain. Quite interestingly, as the adolescent continues to learn and develop the functions listed above, this pre-frontal region initially grows and then begins to shrink. It shrinks as the nerves begin to prune their connections and as a result, become more efficient in processing information. So, to put it lightly, the CEO of the adolescent brain is dynamically growing and learning on the job.

Research shows girls mature through this process up to two years sooner than boys. Most anyone who has worked with groups of young adolescents knows that, in general, girls are typically more aware of the social context of their environment. They inhibit impulses more readily, display better organization and planning and are often more successful within structures like school where these traits are rewarded.

In addition, the emotional center of the brain, known broadly as the limbic system, generates a range of both simple and complex emotions. This system is located behind the pre-frontal area and has nerve pathways connecting them together.

Simple emotions may include anger, as when one is cut off on the highway by another person, or feeling aroused at the sight of an attractive person. Other examples may include those caused by being on the defensive line and seeing your opponent outweigh you by 40 pounds, and stand 5 inches taller. Before the center hikes the ball, he stares at you and says, "I own you. Today you die." Indeed, fear is a powerful basic emotion, as is surprise when you receive the award at a banquet later that year for being the best defensive linesman on the team. The prefrontal lobe seeks to regulate these emotions in a manner consistent with social norms.

Unlike simple emotions, complex emotions are more intricate, such as shame or pride or guilt. These emotions require the frontal lobes to assist in self-evaluation, integrating information from the limbic system.

With basic simple emotions there is a clear physiological response. For example, with anger, the athlete will show an increase in heart rate and blood pressure. This can generally be seen in the tightening of the facial muscles. There can be a change of color in the face and voice tone changes occur in volume and intensity.

Of note, over the years of adolescent development, brain scans show the neural connections between the limbic (emotional) and frontal (CEO) regions of the brain improve and become more efficient. It is not unusual for a 13-year-old to have difficulty managing impulses and with ongoing therapy (such as one may find in a residential program) impulse control becomes more managed. At the same time improvements occur in brain connections that can be seen on brain scans.

While the limbic and pre-frontal connections are becoming more efficient, ongoing therapy can help to assist the CEO-in-training in interpreting emotions, controlling emotions and generating productive, socially appropriate responses to emotions. It has often been said that it is easier to help a delinquent 13-year-old learn to manage mood and behavior than a 17-year-old. That is, the development of prosocial behaviors over time. The research on brain development during adolescence offers us some insight. The frontal lobes' ability to control basic emotions progresses and improves over time, as do the neural pathways connecting the two systems. During this important time, therapy assists with integration and regulation of emotions (limbic) with the executive functions of the prefrontal lobes.

All this information is important within the context of sports as it helps us understand why the young adolescent is in need for a coach to act on occasion as his or her frontal lobes. It comes as no surprise to those who coach young adolescents that more time is spent on regulating athlete impulse, interpreting emotions and helping them to plan and make good decisions. For example, a young athlete displays envy with a statement such as, "They beat us because they have money for good uniforms and equipment." Here the coach can cognitively restructure beliefs with the athlete with a statement such as, "Yes, they have more resources, and they also have more experience than our team, so we will have to work harder than them." This reinterprets the expression of envy, which will not help the team, into a more positive cognition that if we work harder we can beat them.

In my experience, many young adults have looked back at their youth and attribute their success in navigating through a stormy adolescence to a coach. A coach who provides structure, organization and discipline coupled with respect and caring for the adolescent has saved many a young person from the path of self-destruction on which they were headed.

Indeed, as noted previously, on more than one occasion, as a psychologist, I have written orders in an evaluation for a special needs adolescent that they continue in a sport. Schools will often, with good reason, tell a youth they cannot play a sport until their grade point average reaches a certain level. With a special needs adolescent, the current academics may be beyond their ability to succeed. A sport is often the only thing keeping them in school. Also, the coach often has been the level-headed guide in an otherwise confusing world. Regardless of what disarray is occurring in their world, the adolescent can count on the predictability of their sport, team and coach. In addition, the socialization of a healthy team is invaluable to the adolescent.

For this reason and others, good coaches are undervalued in the service to our youth. Also, their role in the overall academic growth of the adolescent is understated. If known by the teachers, aids and administrators, the good coach can help motivate the athlete to increased compliance at school and give feedback about an adolescent's behavior from observations on the field. Knowledge that the adolescent can listen, attend, comply and succeed on the field but cannot do so in the classroom gives the IEP team an additional piece of valuable information in planning the academic program.

Within the context of competition, when the young athlete becomes enraged in a game, you pull the athlete from the game to give them some bench time. It usually does not require much time for them to calm down and then you act as their prefrontal lobes and say something like, "It's ok to feel some anger, but you need to take control and respond to the person who offended you by taking it to the goal. To score points and win the game is the best answer to your opponent's behavior." As this athlete develops in their game they will incorporate your suggestions into their self-talk. As a senior in high school, they may be offended by a member of the opposing team, but say to themselves, "That was a cheap hit. He must be frustrated, and is about to be even more frustrated as I make this goal."

In the scenario with the angry adolescent, the coach has accomplished two goals. First, this young athlete is becoming a better player by being more controlled and directed. Second, this coach is assisting this athlete in learning valuable life skills, which will be a great asset in the future in school or on the job. Well done, coach.

The strategy may be different when at practice and not in a game. Here the coach may remove the athlete and ask them to think about how they may better use their anger, then report back as soon as possible. This self-regulated time out to cognitively process the emotion and restructure the outcome in a socially and game-worthy direction may seem awkward at first but it is more productive than telling the athlete to "Take a lap" or to "Do 30 pushups." Taking a lap as punishment will generally lack the desired outcome for the athlete. As a coach it is very easy to respond to an athlete's anger with anger or frustration of your own, but it lacks a productive immediate outcome, and worse, it teaches the athlete that when they grow up they can control others with anger.

As noted above, complex emotions such as guilt, shame, pride and such are the result of the interaction of the emotional center of the brain and the prefrontal lobes. How these frontal lobes interpret and evaluate emotions is based on learning history, personal temperament and genetics.

As an example of complex emotions, some research indicates embarrassment may involve frontal and temporal lobes and when these are damaged, a person may not appear to experience embarrassment.

For the coach, it is important to note that after Joan's competitor beat her to the goal (a competitor Joan believes has less talent), Joan now feels embarrassed. As the coach approaches her, the embarrassment may become evident to the coach as the athlete does not make eye contact and either looks down to the ground or turns her head away. Often, complex emotions are harder to read in the athlete than simple emotions. This is especially true when an athlete comes from a different culture with different learning histories of how to modulate and present complex feelings.

In Joan's case, the coach has the opportunity to use one of many types of open-ended questions discussed later in this book. For example, a question based on behavior: "What just happened on the field?" Or a question reflecting feeling: "How did that make you feel?" Or one reflecting thoughts: "What do you think just happened that she was able to pass you?" Or they may choose to share empathetically: "I know when that happened to me in the past, I sometimes would feel embarrassed. How do you feel?" They may even try to guide Joan towards a summarization of thoughts and feelings. There are many ways of responding and if you know your athlete you will have an idea which response is best for that situation. Very often, the nonverbal behavior of looking down or away and appearing sullen is sufficient communication and the coach may say, "Okay, you played back-to-back games and she is fresher and not tired now. Hold your head up high and get back in the game. You have more grit and perseverance."

In any of these events, the opportunity to help the young brain of the athlete grow and make better neuronal connections is important in coaching athletes. Developing a better athlete works best when the athlete is well known to the coach and the coach is responding in a manner consistent with her or his comfort level for communicating with this athlete. In the end, it will improve self-talk so the athlete will be better able to cognitively process experiences and feelings to understand and respond to complex emotions.

The literature indicates shame can be a more complex emotion and psychologist Kirsten Weir notes embarrassment is public and, at times, can be laughed off whereas shame is public and private and lacks any sense of humor. An athlete can lose a run to first base and later feel shame that their weight is higher than they desire and blame themselves for "being a pig." Self-shaming is a complex emotion and can be hard for a coach to spot. Shame can become very ingrained in a person and limit their athletic talents as well as seriously affect their health.

In the brain, shame shares many of the same areas as guilt and can be malleable with proper sport specific role modeling. Learning to reinterpret shame may transfer to everyday life and it certainly can make an adolescent a better athlete and help them have a more enjoyable sports experience. Being able to concentrate on the game in the moment and with full attention is compromised by destructive self-thoughts of shame or guilt. These emotions also tighten muscles, making one a less competitive athlete.

The adolescent brain is also bathed in neurochemicals that can facilitate a sense of reward, punishment and such things as risk taking behavior. Given that reasoning centers, emotional centers and interconnections are all developing and pruning for efficiency, neurochemical regulation adds to the many challenges for the young athlete. The brain of the young athlete is much more likely than the adult to experience heightened reward and pleasure in risk taking behavior. Also, the athlete experiences a much greater biological reward when the risk is taken in a group setting.

One example of controlled risk taking I have observed is during our long marathon group training runs was in the winter. Part of the course involves running across a frozen lake. Frozen lakes often make creaking sounds and the runners have usually believed they were taking risks running across the lake. Truth be known, none of these runs were ever taken across an unknown lake where water current could affect ice thickness. Also, it was never taken with thickness under 10 inches. But since the truth was not completely known to these athletes, the lake crossing experience left the group with a powerful sense of accomplishment and greater bonding with each other. The pleasure center of the brain was reinforced for that "risk." I have done this with rope swings in rivers and hill sliding, but all with the knowledge the risk was controlled even though the runners may not have thought the risk was under control. At reunions, the athletes recall these events with great fondness.

Beyond the study of development and regulation of emotions in the brain is the fascinating area of mirror nerve cells in the brain. Early research in brain scans showed there are nerve cells that activate when engaged in an action such as grasping an object, and they also activate when observing another person grasp an object. This occurs when the observer intends to subsequently grasp the object. This phenomenon of learning by observing yielded a wonderful area of study in investigating these mirror neurons. This has many implications for the biology of social learning without actually engaging in the behavior.

As time progressed and brain scans yielded more and better information and studies became more complex in design, it became evident that many areas of the brain respond in a symphony in what has become known as 'action understanding.' That is, the brain can interpret—mirror—the action of another and replicate that action, and there are cells that respond when simply observing the behavior with intention to replicate that behavior. Also, many areas of the brain are involved when observing the behavior with the intention to engage following that observation.

Given this information, like most areas of human learning and behavior, some people are better able to observe and replicate than other people. For example, with verbal learning, some people can open an anatomy text and read it once in preparation for an exam while others struggle to learn the mnemonic for the 12 cranial nerves. Academic learning follows a normal distribution with some people being more efficient in learning and others less efficient.

Action understanding follows a similar distribution with some more people being more skilled than others at learning through mirroring. This is evident if you have ever taken a group dance lesson. The individual learning differences become quite apparent.

For the person having difficulty with action understanding, they may have difficulty when learning from training videos that are taken at the mid-field side line. They may do best with the camera behind them recording from the perspective most familiar to their observations. Game day videos, if used solely for the opportunity to shame players as a group after a loss, can be viewed from anywhere since the" learning" is purely emotional and aversive, not visual-spatial, for the purpose of sensory motor integration and execution.

Like most anything else, practice allows the nerves in the brain to consolidate and retain the information so that later, for example, the basketball player won't have to think about dribbling the ball and can concentrate on the game. In learning, a cell phone responsibly used can be a good teaching instrument. The athlete can take short practice videos at home to email to their coach. That can provide baseline information and progress as well as serve as a powerful motivator for the athlete to maintain compliance and demonstrate improvements towards their goals on a weekly basis. As well, the coach can offer specific email or in person recommendations based on the video.

As a side note, it may be interesting to ask an athlete who their favorite athlete is in their sport so you can see how they are attempting to mimic that athlete's behavior. As example I had a young sprinter who modeled an athlete from the early days when tracks were cinder and dirt. In those days, the athlete would use a trowel to dig a small hole for foot placement. Prior to the start they would get in a 'ready' position and kick back to shake off any dirt that may have been on their racing shoes. The athlete I coached incorporated that behavior without explanation or understanding of its roots. Also, another of his models would run very fast and maintain acceleration beyond 70 meters where many would begin to fall apart. However, that model had a habit of coming out of the blocks almost fully upright on the second step. This athlete did the same, but would over stride on the second and third steps resulting in deceleration on those steps. Convincing him required borrowing his cell phone to video his exit from the blocks and then showing him in slow motion how his foot went too far forward, slowing him down while he was attempting to accelerate. Fortunately, in this case, logic and science trumped beloved sprinting heroes.

Top tier athletes are trained based on their body structure. What works for one person may require adjustments for another athlete. For example, swimmer Michael Phelps has an advantaged body structure. He completes a 200-meter medley in 1 minute and 54.66 seconds. He worked hard to attain this incredible goal and had some assist with a wingspan of 6.66 feet, double-jointed elbows, and other wonderful physical advantages. Michael Jordan at his peak had a vertical leap of 48." Larry Bird had a vertical of 28." The training and development of their basketball techniques to gain advantages over opponents were necessarily different, as would have to be any of the athletes trying to mimic them with individual bodies of their own.

How, for example, might this affect your feedback to an athlete with a love of and emulation of Larry Bird's 3-point shots to basket with minimal elevation off the court? Does it matter that your athlete has a personal vertical leap of 45"? Knowing who the hero is in a young athlete's life tells you who they are observing and likely modeling, and depending on their own physique their brains may be responding to and learning techniques that may disadvantage them; and once learned, this behavior may take a long time to correct.

As noted above, as the adolescent learns, the brain grows and becomes more efficient. When we consider the functioning of humans and animals in their environment, the brain's primary role is in searching for food, reproduction and responding to danger. Thus, anthropologically there is an evolved need for rapid and integrated responses if the human is to survive. Consider the example of two cavemen in a field enjoying a quiet spring afternoon when they spot a large predator approaching them. One caveman runs into the field and the second caveman runs to a cave. The caveman in the field becomes lunch and the one in the cave observes his successful survival facilitated by fleeing to the cave. To survive in the future, he must learn from this success.

Since movement is required for sustenance, reproduction and survival, it should come as no great surprise that learning occurs best when the organism is in motion or has recently been in motion. Studies substantiate that during the motion of running, and for a period of time after, the brain is best able to learn and remember information. In fact, what we have come to learn is during and following aerobic work, the brain produces a protein called brain derived neurotrophic factor (BDNF). John Ratey, M.D., in his recent book *Spark: The Revolutionary New Science of Exercise and the Brain,* refers to BDNF as fertilizer (Hyponex) for the brain. With elevations of BDNF the brain produces new brain cells and new connections between cells. As BDNF increases, so does learning. During recent years we have seen an explosion of research in this area of study. Following an aerobic exercise, academic performance improves, mood improves, sleep is more regulated and ability to maintain attention and focus improves for the person.

This would certainly seem to be good news for coaches and for teachers, and should also serve as a caution to certain school districts that have eliminated student recess from their daily schedules. Notably, Ratey's book documents incredible academic improvements among the students at Naperville school which were made following morning exercise within their tolerances. Ratey has reported people reducing or eliminating antidepressants and anxiolytics following a regimen of aerobic work.

This knowledge led me to develop research with students in our Exercise and Sport Psychology class. Students in the classes ranged from highly competitive intercollegiate athletics to sedentary students whose interests went in a different direction than sports. All students wore a heart rate monitor during the morning exercise and had to demonstrate a heart rate in the range of 130 to 160 unless there was a health concern. The class is a Tuesday/Thursday class held at 8:30 AM and the students would come for a 20-minute workout at 7 AM. Initially, there was much grumbling, but through the course of the semester students came to enjoy the social activity that included an aerobic event.

The heart rate monitor was important as each person is different physically and has a different baseline heart rate. Two students exemplified this difference. A sedentary student was walking and talking during the exercise and the initial impression was that he was not taking the exercise seriously. A check of his heart rate revealed a high 180— slow down or do interval walking. A second student was a cross country runner who was running at what appeared a comfortably quick pace yet her heart rate was a modest 140.

The student with a 180 would be doomed to eventual injury and come not to enjoy exercising if he had been encouraged to continuously exercise at a heart rate of 180.

As a result, when divided into an exercise and non-exercise group, students who exercised reported greater perceived academic self-efficacy and a more positive mood for the 8:30 class. This observation continued when groups were reversed.

Also, it is important to note that in competitive sports, exercise is targeted and directed with great specificity. The athlete has a workout schedule that can be quite tedious. The pre-class activity was made to be social and fun in nature with an eye on maintaining a mild to moderate aerobic heart rate.

Recently, students assisted in summer research with a group of elderly participants. On the first day group A was the experimental group and B the control group and the next day experimental and control groups switched roles. A number of mood measures and neuropsychological measures of verbal and nonverbal learning were administered. One group would walk for 20 minutes at their normal exercise walking pace and the second group received a lecture on volunteerism by a high energy and motivating speaker. Groups were reversed the next day. Blood samples of BDNF were taken and both blood samples and psychological testing was done pre and post activities.

This was a small study with a small sample. However, there were some minimal, but significant cognitive differences noted with the elderly showing increased BDNF, indicating a selective cognitive benefit of activity. It should be noted the walkers did maintain a 120 to 140 heart rate but were instructed to walk based on their normal exercise exertion and not attend to heart rate. Student research investigators recorded heart rate.

Given that learning occurs best following exercise and given exercise improves mood, facilitates normal sleep and assists with attentional focus, it is reasonable to structure practices to have heart rate based warm ups until the athletes learn to base heart rate on exertion. You do not want to fatigue athletes before or following practice unless it has a practice-intended effect. Generally, it is recommended that it be a 20-minute warm up. But whatever can be done is better than nothing. For a football center, a fast-paced exercise walk to practice may be appropriate for him as his focus is more on resistance exercise than aerobics. However, linemen on a football team without aerobic work may not be functioning at their best. It is recommended this activity be pleasant, not regimented.

It is also well known that sleep two nights prior to a big game is more important than the night prior to the game. It is on these days that an easy 20-minute cool down may best benefit the athlete if it is not too late in the day.

While it may seem illogical to ask a golfer to take a run, the heart rate specific activity, in addition to its biological benefits, can become an enjoyable lifestyle benefit that persists long after the team uniforms are put away. If this exercise is fun (for example, taking a light jog with someone you just met) and not targeted for high workload (e.g. 45 seconds up the hill, take heart rate, jog down, record heart rate at the bottom and at a recovery heart rate of 120 continue the hill run, repeating until your time up the hill begins to get you less distance than your starting run up the hill) you likely will continue this exercise. While the latter may be great during a specific time of a season of competition, the former is likely to become part of a lifestyle.

Also, it is common for students to do better academically during their sport's season. This can be partially attributed to a number of things, but certainly the aerobic work is part of it. Further, offseason runs facilitate continued positive brain development.

Note that while it is clear BDNF helps with academic success, it is also a benefit to the coach who is attempting to teach playbook to the athletes. If a workout is too hard the learning can be clouded by sleepiness. A moderate workout allows for improved learning and focus. Also, many coaches know athletes are more relaxed after a workout and in a better position to receive difficult emotional news such as, "Mike, I know you were QB in high school but we need you as a tight end."

One other factor here is when the body is in a heightened state of physical activity, it releases a stress hormone called cortisol. This hormone assists the body during a fight or flight or flock response to threat. It can be produced when a person is highly anxious, leaving the body ready to fight or flee even when there is no objective physical threat in sight, rather a foreboding exam in school or the stress of solo living during a pandemic. A very anxious person can produce cortisol when no objective threat is present and this can support unintended weight gain. Running can assist in managing cortisol. Therefore aerobic activity increases BDNF, facilitating learning, and helps manage cortisol and therefore the person may experience feeling less anxious and ready for the challenge at hand.

The effects of exercise are quite observable in an injured athlete who cannot be active. Without elevated activity, he or she generally becomes anxious, grumpy and mildly depressed. Within less than two weeks after an injury the biochemistry of the athlete changes, so there is a biological reason for their negative mood which is in addition to the social and sports related loss. As a result, this athlete is also prone to quit the team unless on full scholarship.

It's important to keep the injured athlete engaged and active. If, for example, they cannot run then they can ride a stationary bike. If not a bike, then a rowing machine. If not rowing then aquatic jogging. If it is a metabolic issue and the athlete has to be sedentary, they need to be kept engaged with the team. This helps minimize the negative biological effects of abrupt cessation of aerobic activity.

While I do not offer information here on nutrition, healthy nutrition is very important in brain development. In general, without a registered dietician as a consultant, a preseason written recommendation of healthy eating options pre and post exercise and developed by a licensed professional is suggested.

Finally, one can't discuss athletes' brains without treating the issue in athletics that has come to such prominence in the last decade or so: concussions. Sports teams have specific rules for what to do when a concussion is suspected. The value of accurate diagnoses cannot be understated. A second concussion closely tied to a first concussion in time can result in death. We also know that multiple concussions have a serious effect on brain function in later years of life.

In my experience we undervalue concussions that are not dramatic in occurrence. A loud crashing of the helmets with the intensity of two rams butting heads gets immediate attention. A young female athlete who heads the ball in a soccer game and acts dizzy for a moment is less dramatic, but she cannot be left unattended. The response of, "She must be fine, it was just a header and she was dizzy for a minute but says she is okay now," represents dangerous thinking. This adolescent must be assessed by a training staff and communication must be made with the parents. We know that it is not unusual for this athlete to complain of mild symptoms at home and then at practice, to assure her place on the team and show grit in front of her teammates, say she is fine.

I once knew a Division I football player who was told that after three concussions he could no longer play football. I also knew a DI female soccer player who said, "I have had seven concussions and I still play soccer." It is possible that we don't take a woman's trauma in sports as seriously as we do a man's trauma. Further, unless there is a clear protocol, it is easy for an athlete to hide their injuries. It is easier to miss a concussion from a hard header to a soccer ball than hearing the loud crashing of helmets. While these are just observations without a strong literature base, it is important to proceed cautiously when it comes to concussions. Even, for example, when someone with a history of concussions leaves a sport known for concussions to an endurance sport where they might dehydrate over long runs, it is best to get medical clearance for safe entry into the new sport.

Varsity sport college students take a baseline neuropsychological screen coming into college sports. I have overheard students say, "Don't do too well because if you get a concussion it will be hard to return to practice." As this tool progresses in time it will continue to have improvements that challenge the ability to fake a weak baseline score.

The athlete with a concussion will stop physical activities until medically cleared and should stop academic work, but the latter is not always practical. Therefore, initially, they may require accommodations such as studying in daylight or incandescent light and avoiding 60 cycle per second fluorescent light while they complain of vision or headache concerns. Also, early in the day while the brain is fresh is the best time to study, and study should be broken into smaller intervals, about 20 minutes, with short breaks.

Based on my history as a psychologist, I have known depressed and anxious injured athletes who complain of not being cleared to play months after being taken out of their sport. In consult with one athlete, I discovered the depression and anxiety were associated with being out of her sport, inactive, and away from her friends on the team, and suffering mild sleep concerns. The headaches had changed from the typical concussion headache to a musculoskeletal headache. Her poor testing scores were associated with wanting to pass the test so badly she would cognitively freeze due to anxiety and fail the test. In this instance she was referred to a neurologist for final clearance, whereupon the tension-related headaches went away and joy returned.

Clearly, no trainer would return an athlete to practice with poor scores and headaches. The point is there is still much to learn about concussion management among athletes. This is especially so with the female athlete and the adolescent athlete. All our brains are fragile and vulnerable, and the adolescent brain is especially so. The good news is that whether it be in the area of concussions, nutrition, exercise, or cognitive development, we know more today about the workings of our bodies than we ever have, and as coaches we can use this knowledge to help protect our athletes, help them succeed in their sport, and most importantly cultivate in them lifelong habits for cognitive and physiological health.

Now I turn to the workings of what some refer to as the wholistic brain, often described as "mind." That aspect of the developing self that is structuring meaning intellectually, emotionally and relationally based on their experiences directly and through observing others.

THREE

SELF-FULFILLING PROPHECY AND THE TWO FACES OF MINDFULNESS

W hat does it mean to be Mindful?

Most often, when the topic of mindfulness is discussed, it is associated with meditation. Early research on meditation in the United States was conducted by Herbert Benson, M.D. His research reported that meditation fundamentally requires three things: a quiet environment, a relaxed posture and a passive attitude. Mindful meditation has come to be known as being present in the moment, being aware of feelings and thoughts in a nonjudgmental manner. This mindfulness is associated with the practice of meditation.

Practicing this mindfulness for a specified period of time affords many personal benefits that are documented in the literature. John Kabat-Zinn is a current example of a leader in this practice. The reader is encouraged to see his YouTube videos, which offer excellent examples of mindful meditation and its benefits.

For mindful meditation to be effective it takes consistency and time, and while one or two young athletes may be consistent practitioners, for a team to practice becomes a challenge due to noncompliance. I know this statement invites criticism from practitioners, but in my experience, when meditation is assigned to a group, there is generally considerable noncompliance out of season, which is unfortunate. But we know that it's hard to get athletes to do plyometrics on their own or even gentle stretching. Given the young athlete is poor at these basic physical disciplines, adding meditation is indeed a challenge.

One thing I have found in my coaching that can work well is combining targeted active yoga with a brief meditation included at the end. Here, depending on where you are in the season, you can emphasize stretching or strengthening followed with brief meditation and include an image of self-awareness focused on the day of competition.

A good yoga instructor can be a great assist for emphasizing strengthening early in the season, stretching later in the season (though of course we do both throughout) and elements of mindfulness specific to the sport, which the yoga instructor can introduce to the practice in consultation with the coach. In our practice I have participated with the yoga instructor and the team. Along with the instructor I would include imagery of day of competition. This imagery would include awareness of environment (visual, auditory, kinesthetic images) in an attempt to assist the athlete to control race day emotional and physical arousal so it is at an optimal level for competition.

While many will say they have no funds for yoga, there are many instructors who would love to build their resume by assisting a sports team. It is important to get an instructor who can adapt to seasonal needs of the team and work collaboratively with the coach.

This focus on mindfulness is what is commonly thought of when the term is discussed. However, there is a different form of mindfulness, which is quite important in maximizing the likelihood of victory and enhancing the growth of the athlete. I call this the second face of mindfulness.

Ellen Langer, Professor of Psychology at Harvard University, basically defines mindfulness as being actively engaged in the present, having a flexible state of mind, and the capacity to notice new things. The YouTube example if this is a good primer for this section. See, YouTube "Let's talk about mindfulness: An interview with Ellen Langer."

Similar to a parent saying "Be mindful of what you are doing," you are being asked to attend to the matter at hand and be present in the moment. In addition to paying attention to what is occurring, we are also being encouraged to have a flexible state of mind. As an example, in Langer's research in the 1970s she studied a group of men who spent a week surrounded with items of their past and were instructed to live in the past, 20 years ago, and only to speak and act in that time frame. The control group only discussed the past but was not immersed in the past. By the end of the study the experimental group, by immersing themselves in the past, heightened their awareness of a younger self and they showed improvements in hearing, eyesight, mobility and dexterity.

Clearly our physical limitations are affected by our self-perceptions. And while there are certainly limits (regardless of how hard I may try, I cannot will myself to fly), we tend not to push the limits of our own capabilities and we often accept the limitations society unintentionally places on us. For example, if I see myself as frail (with age it is not at all unusual to wake up with some aches and pains), I may not exercise each day. However, daily exercise increases heart rate and respiration, has positive effects on the immune system, facilitates regulation of normal sleep and generates the release of BDNF in the brain. It would not be difficult to find someone who would say, "At your age, you deserve to rest," potentially reinforcing a self-perception of being frail.

It is important to note that, whether or not we are self-aware, others are mindful of us, and if we are unaware of their actions toward us we can set limitations that affect our potential and even our health. We clearly see this when, early in the season, athletes establish a hierarchy or pecking order among themselves. When someone is seen as, for example, a great foul shooter, and someone else as a poor foul shooter, they tend to accommodate the perceptions. We all tend to live up to others' expectations of us and become internally mindful of ourselves as very good or below average.

Another example is when an elderly person is told out of kindness, "Let me get that for you," "Do you need help with the computer?" "Let me get the door," "Should someone your age be doing that?" The person may begin to self-limit activities as they accept the kind assistance of others, and in doing so facilitate frailty's progression. The kindness of others is wonderful and should be rewarded, but as we become more mindful of ourselves we see our real physical potential. For example, a 100-year-old man running the marathon under 8:30, or Katherine Switzer, the first woman to run the Boston Marathon in 1966, or Julia Hawking, who in 2019 at the age of 103 competed in the 100-meter dash in the Senior Games.

To say this is just genetics is to deny our capacity. Yes, genetics sets the limits of our envelope but not how far we can push to the boundaries of the envelope. Many people never explore those limits and are not mindful of others' limiting beliefs about themselves. Mindfulness helps us develop our full potential by developing our ability to be fully self-aware in our world.

Social pressure to conform to stereotypes of course is very strong. In a recent presentation to a group, a gentleman in his mid-80s lamented his cross country skiing activities. When asked why, he replied, "I cannot find anyone my age to ski with." Since he has lost peer athletes to join him in his sport, he is perceived as acting out of the norm and is perceived as atypical or unusual, whereas for him personally, skiing is not an unusual activity at all.

Another elderly gentleman noted his friends who walk the golf course are on fewer meds than those who ride the golf carts. Granted those riding may have health conditions (outside their physical envelope) that have caused them to forego walking, but riding may also reaffirm their mindset of being impaired. Is it possible to ride but to stop the cart more distant from the green than usual? Also, the men walking have a mindset of being 'healthy' and may have personal attributions of more healthy lifestyles, which can affect to some extent choices such as diet and non-golf related activities. On a personal note, when I was young and ran a marathon family and friends would ask, "What was your time?" Somewhere after entering my late 50s they stopped asking my time and would simply say something like, "That is amazing, good for you," indicating they were sufficiently impressed that I could actually run a marathon at my age regardless of time to completion.

Mindfulness and Young Athletes:
CASES IN POINT

Using the simplified description of Langer's mindfulness, which includes engagement in the present, active state of mind, and capacity to notice new things, I turn now specifically to the young athlete, and offer what I believe are some common examples that illustrate the difference mindfulness can make.

1. **Example:** During the summer the athlete makes decisions in bed in the morning such as, "I have to work today. I have a summer running schedule but maybe I will do it after work though I know I will work late today." The athlete then feels mild guilt and resolves that guilt with the belief that "I am a good athlete, but not really as good as so and so, besides I don't really believe coach will play me anyhow. I am not even sure coach likes me." **Suggestion:** Before summer break, the coach encourages this athlete and all the others *not to make decisions in bed* (never a good idea). Rather, the coach has instructed them, "Get up, put on your running shoes and gear then head out of the house to the corner. If when standing on the corner you find you just don't have it on that day, go back to bed and know you needed the rest." Once geared up, athletes stay in that present moment of being an athlete rather than the moment of being a bed head. They are in a different present moment than being in the house. Also, having assigned buddies who check in on

each other in a positive manner is very valuable. As with study groups, you just need to be sure you have the right combination of buddies.

2. **Example:** Years ago I noticed a team having dinner about three hours before a game. This team had athletes who consistently played in games, some who played on an intermittent basis, and athletes who consistently rode the bench. Casual observation revealed an occasional athlete who was not anticipating playing in the game was eating considerably more food and heavier food (fats, carbs) than the starters. They were all experiencing the same world but with a different mindfulness of self. **Suggestion:** This difference in food consumption reflected the athletes' different perceptions of themselves relative to their coach and team culture. And it is impossible to know how much the indulgent eating was a cause or effect of the limited playtime or vice versa, but that the two were related seemed clear. It certainly was a sign of a mindful self-awareness, be it transitional ("I failed a test today and feel terrible") or enduring ("I will never play so why not eat what comforts me?"). Also, it may be an advantage for the coach to discuss this athlete's expectations regarding play time to see how well expectations may or may not match those of the coach.

3. **Example:** For the last three years this team has always beat us in the final period of our hockey game. They have better athletes and are better

funded and have better support systems. Their parents have a huge booster group and we don't even have our own rink or skate sharpening equipment. **Suggestion:** This recurring defeat in the final period becomes a self-fulfilling prophecy. The error is in the strong focus on the game outcome (and then by consequence the apparent advantages the other team has) rather than the game process. As coach you look at reasons for third period loss, but with the athlete, you need to help them process and focus on objectives for the third period and not on the outcome objective of winning the game. Being mindful of game process, directed by the coach, advantages the players to become mindful of their potential and enhances the likelihood of a win. Process goals specific to the athlete and team are important, especially when there is a mindset of expectation of a final period loss . For example, in the case of a 100 meter athlete with a goal of dropping 2/10th of a second off her time, the goal is laudable, but does not help to reset a mindful attitude because it belongs in the distant future. Working instead on a meet goal of, for example, improving how she takes the first three steps out of the blocks, with specific instruction, gives her a sense of success and readjusts her self-statements, giving her more flexibility in how she views herself as an athlete.

Further, it has been my philosophy that to change a mindset it is easiest for the athletes to first believe in the coach and then transition to a belief in themselves. This comes from my practice as a psychologist where clients come to treatment because they don't know how to change themselves. First they develop a belief in their therapist's skills and talents and then incorporate it into a belief that they can do it now and hopefully in the future.

4. **Example:** A competitor gives one of your athletes a cheap hit during a basketball game and your athlete becomes angry and you can see his focus is now shifted to his sense of finding personal justice. **Suggestion:** I am sure you have already anticipated this suggestion. You need to make the athlete work in the present, envision a different and more flexible approach, so you call a time out and with a stern look say to the athlete, "I know you are upset, answer by taking it to the hoop not to the person." We don't think of this as a valuable life lesson but it is a critical lesson at a young age. Stay focused, stay in the present, be mindful of yourself in the moment and you may meet your goal. This example is easily transferred to the eventual adult working in any professional environment.

5. **Example:** An athlete is consistently a 90% shooter from the foul line and in the past 4 games has dropped to 60% with 40% during critical game moments. **Suggestion:** Assuming no physical injury or acute environmental issue (such as death of a loved one or dad never comes to games but

has been to the last 5 games) it is time to review the athlete's change in mindful activity.

Societal pressure from others or an authority can be sufficient to make an athlete or any person second guess and limit physical activity. This will have a degrading effect on the body and shift one's mindfulness to that of, "I am old and need to act my age," or, "I'm a lousy free-throw shooter." The effect on young athletes may actually be worse than upon an older person because they seek approval during a continued development of self in relation to others.

A shift in confidence can destroy the natural rhythm of the free throw when "being in the moment" changes. Specifically, the athlete has said to herself, "I am good at this," then positions her left foot at the line, right foot a bit back, dribbles 2 times, rolls her shoulders once, looks at the hoop, shoots and *swish*. Now the athlete says to herself, "I used to be good at this; I will just do my best, but I don't think so," then without realizing it, her self-talk tightens her shoulders just enough, takes her history of consistent rhythm away and she throws an air ball or throws too hard, further reaffirming her mindfulness of self as not a good athlete who may then avoid teammates after the game and isolate in her room.

Indeed, there was once a competing coach who assisted my athlete to a win in a distance run. My athlete was about 700 meters from completing an 8k run and a competing athlete was gradually closing in on him. The competing coach ran up to his athlete and hollered, "You got him! He is nothing! He is no one! Now beat him!" My athlete kicked in just enough to convince his competitor he would not pass and took the win. My athlete later reported, "Coach, I had nothing, I was hanging in but when I heard that coach I forgot I had nothing and knew he [his competition] would not pass me."

This is a good example of being in the moment instead of thinking of distance to the finish line and shifting cognitions from "I am dead" to "He won't beat me." I frequently speak to distance athletes about strategies to reset competitors' beliefs about their ability to pass an athlete. A simple one in a long run is to take 5 quick steps after a turn where you are not visible to the competition. The distance is not so great as to reveal the strategy but just enough to have competition wonder if they can keep up. Here the athlete shifts mindfulness from "I don't have it to the finish line" to "Ok, I will take some quick steps around that corner and I am tired but my strategy will give me an advantage." The athlete is focused on the moment and shifts from a negative cognition to an active positive cognition in the moment.

Coaching moment to moment based on the athlete's abilities and unique personality is indeed a challenge. Adjusting state of mind in the moment is made more feasible by having the athlete journal self-talk that occurred during an event and do so immediately following the event, and by now and then assisting the athlete to shift self-talk. Here, a coach consultation with a Sports Psychologist can be very helpful.

For the basketball player mentioned above, modifying self-talk and using mindful meditation for specific transfer to a game appropriate muscle tension will help reset mindfulness of "I used to be an athlete" to "Wow, that was a slump, glad it is behind me."

By practicing mindful meditation in this instance, she is taught to combine breathing with gentle muscle tension and relaxation to be aware of slight increases in tension returning to game level tension. Next, at the end of this practice she breathes out while making a sub-vocal sound of *shhhhh* (or whatever she prefers), which is intended to interfere with negative self-talk and act as a cue to let go of her elevated tension and return to her foul shot ritual and rhythm.

This works when there is a belief and trust by the athlete in the coach and others working with her. Again, the process is made specific to the individual based on their journaling or discussion of self-talk and reviewed with practice. This practice is first done alone, then in team practice, then in a game when it is not at a critical time. Here, consistent with mindful awareness of your athlete, you have the athlete trust you before she trusts in her ability to effect a change. You are helping the athlete to "be in the moment" in the game and helping her with her mindful awareness of self as an athlete playing in the present (not in a mental self-talk) and in the rhythm of the moment of the game.

While it is certainly ideal to have a Sports Psychologist or similar practitioner, many do not have this resource available. As noted with the example of a yoga instructor described above, there are young practitioners who would donate time to a team for the good of the community and for building their resume.

For the coach to assist the athlete it is important to appraise and modify how the athlete is distracted from competing in the present moment. This is needed to maintain cognitive flexibility to respond to rapidly changing game dynamics and to notice new things on the court or field of play.

Once again, the use of this training with the athlete has later life implications in managing challenging situations. Good coaching is good teaching and instills valuable life lessons.

SELF-FULFILLING PROPHECY

In the 1960s, two researchers, Robert Rosenthal and Lenore Jacobson, conducted research, which became known as the Pygmalion Effect. These researchers took a group of elementary school students and gave them an intelligence test. They then took some of the students who took the test and told their teachers they showed strong potential for intellectual growth and would blossom within the year. In fact, these students were simply randomly selected without having demonstrated these traits as a group. By the end of the year, these students scored significantly higher than their fellow students. When the teachers believed the prophecy that the students would excel, the students met their expectations.

For this to happen the teachers had to believe their students were gifted and then modify their behavior toward the students. In turn, the students had to believe what the teachers were saying and how the teachers acted toward them. In addition, the students had to believe the teachers were credible in their appraisal of the students.

In coaching, the self-fulfilling prophecy has many implications. Credibility of the coach is often accepted de facto with the title of "coach." Indeed, over the years I have been impressed at just how much the athlete will believe in the coach, at times often to the athlete's disadvantage. An example is the student who says, "I can never be a good sprinter as I don't have explosive power." This was a response to a coach who measured jump height and suggested the athlete focus on distance over sprint. The coach who would attempt to change the belief of the student would have to have credibility. Credibility can be established by giving the athlete small goals in jump height that are challenging and attainable along with practice and providing measurable results.

Having written this, it must be noted that athletes often need to be gently moved in the direction of demonstrated physical talent, meaning your best 5k runners are generally not your best jumpers. Further, the young athlete who is deeply passionate about jumps, whose body is not fully developed as yet and who has no interest or love for distance running is best to pursue their enthusiasm for jumping, while being encouraged to do some distance practice to see if their interest develops over time. However, if the coach is fully focused on the win with very young athletes, the drive to win may pressure the coach to insist the athlete change their enthusiasms. It takes a confident and quality coach to redirect an athlete's passion.

Given that the athlete is inclined to believe in their coach, self-fulfilling prophecy may come into play. One great example is the area of college recruiting. If you listen to walk-on athletes on a college team where other athletes have scholarship money, you will find that these walk-on athletes believe they have to work harder to get their coach's attention. When you ask why that is so, the athlete will express their belief that the coach invested time, effort and money to secure the scholarship athlete and therefore has a clear bias toward that athlete. To see a coach discipline a recruited athlete with scholarship money for missing the execution of a pattern in football, whereas the walk-on athlete is told "nice effort" is to understand their point. Such differences are not missed by athletes in either category. The walk-on athlete generally knows they are not special in the eyes of the coach. If the athlete does not quickly resolve the discrepancy, then they are likely to start responding in a manner that confirms the belief that they are only average or less than average.

An example of self-fulfilling prophecy in my own life came with a basic cardiovascular health measure. As one ages the heart rate charts diminish from an average maximum heart rate of around 200 at age 20 to 155 at age 65. As I aged, and continued to run, loved ones who are in the medical profession would tell me that my heart rate should be well below 150, and yet I attained 180 with elevated exertion but not sprint speed. I started to believe I should be "mindful" of my age and slow down, thereby reinforcing the old man prophecy.

That was until I reviewed the research. The heart rate charts are based on a cross sectional analysis of people. However, when Jack Daniels, PhD, (a highly respected physiologist, researcher, teacher and coach) conducted a longitudinal study, the results were different. Daniels studied endurance athletes from the 1968 Olympics, investigating maximum heart rates and then followed up with them 40+ years later. When studying specific individuals over time, rather than a cross section of individuals, he found only about a 2 beat difference in maximum heart rate, not a 45 beat difference. This assisted me in my mindset of healthy aging and not accepting a self-fulfilling prophecy of a normal heart rate that was well below my own individual, healthy heartbeat. Again, similar to Langer's research, awareness of self as one who cannot or should not do something is a mindful state that can become very limiting. Clearly, there are limitations that come with age and a shrinking of the physical envelope of capability, but when we self-limit further than that, we do so at our own peril.

One other example is that of gender. For many years school books were written with emphasis (sometimes exclusive) on the male gender. Young girls were given the message that science was the exclusive domain of boys. For example, "The biologist and *his* colleagues in chemistry..." This provided the effect of suggesting to girls that science was not their domain. In athletics, prior to 1967 it was believed a woman's body could not tolerate the trauma of running a marathon and many fulfilled this prophecy by simply accepting it until Katherine Switzer stole her way into the Boston Marathon and became the first woman to run the marathon. Today there is now a debate whether women are physiologically *better* suited to run the ultra-marathon (100 mile event) than are men.

Closely related to self-fulfilling prophecy is something known as *confirmation bias*. Here a person has a preconceived bias (perhaps coming from effects of a coach's self-fulfilling prophecy) and uses this bias to validate their preconceptions.

A sophomore basketball player shoots 67% from the foul line and has the preconceived notion that he is good and improving. On his next free throw he misses and says to himself, "That is too bad, I will keep working on it," whereas his friend has a 67% free throw percentage, but a preconceived notion that "I am a walk-on and I know the coach does not think I am very good," despite the fact the coach never said anything beyond nonverbal indications. Here, following a missed shot this player says to himself, "Wow, I am not very good and my parents are at this game." The coach unwittingly, through his own self-fulfilling prophecy, set a standard for the young walk-on and now this young athlete is using a developing confirmation bias to prove to himself he is less than average even while his free-throw percentage is identical to that of his friend.

Granted there are people who come to a team with a global optimistic view of themselves and some with a global negative view of themselves, both based on their particular developmental history. Because every person is different, assisting the young athlete even while trying to be cognizant of one's own biases is indeed a challenging task.

Once again, for the young athlete, keeping a journal of game related thoughts and feelings following the game can be very valuable. However, reviewing the journals with the athlete should never be judgmental and not shared with the team. Rather if the coach can discuss the journal with the athlete, emphasizing positive elements and how to shift self-talk on game days, the exercise can have a very positive effect. In doing this, the coach is seeking to cognitively restructure (there is a formal therapeutic approach known as cognitive restructuring) the athlete's irrational or maladaptive thoughts and emotions to a more positive direction. Also the coach can use this information to discuss the athlete's development with a mentor or trusted fellow coach. This can help determine where the coach's own biases occur, biases that can influence the athlete's self-attributions with its possible effects on the coach's perception his or her athlete.

Consider one final example. Jan, Diane's sister, always runs the 100-meter event at .5 to 1.5 seconds slower than her sister. Her coach has told Jan that Diane is faster than her and has told Diane she is one of the best athletes she has coached in this event. Given the coach's biases leading to the self-fulfilling prophecy of which sister is fastest, the sister adopted the coach's attitude and engaged in separate confirmation biases, one being helpful and the other not helpful. Then her new high school coach had Jan journal her thoughts and feelings immediately before and after the event and was able to identify thoughts and feelings that were confirming Jan's bias. From there, she was able to gently dispute her maladaptive thoughts and facilitate a shift in thoughts and feelings while in combination with a training program to help Jan improve her event time.

SUMMARY

Mindfulness can have a powerful impact on an athlete's performance as well as their long-term self-perception and development. The two faces of mindfulness include one focused on a meditative process where one is in a quiet place with a relaxed posture (usually sitting) and regulating breathing while taking a passive attitude (not holding onto thoughts that come to mind) and being in the moment. It is effective if practiced consistently, but compliance by the athlete can be a challenge. Alternatively, using yoga focused on the athlete specific to strength, flexibility and self-awareness coupled with a meditative component may have many advantages to the athlete and the team.

Langer's mindfulness involves being in the present, having a flexible state of mind and having and an openness to new things. This is valuable in assisting the athlete to their best performance in adjusting cognitions and feelings relative to their game development and progression. Add to this the self-fulfilling prophecy by the coach and acceptance by the athlete, and we have a recipe for athletes developing confirmation biases which can enhance or limit their development. Journaling of thoughts and feelings before and after a game can be a very valuable exercise in assisting the coach to identify areas where the athlete could benefit from help with restructuring dysfunctional thoughts. Through the gentle disputing of maladaptive thoughts and feelings the athlete can grow beyond self-imposed limits and unjust biases to reach their full potential. In the process this athlete will also have become a more self-aware individual, who may well serve as an empathetic teacher, coach or mentor to future athletes.

FOUR

COACH AS TEACHER AND STUDENT

THE COACH AS A STUDENT

Whether coaching a town soccer team, a junior high school tennis team or an Olympic biathlon, as a coach you are forever a student of your sport. And this is the life of any teacher. Most people would be incredulous if a college professor, or a seasoned teacher at any level, declared they knew all there was to know in their subject and no longer needed to expand their knowledge.

Recall from Chapter 1 my experiences in observing and talking with Hall of Fame coaches. These coaches are at the very top of their sport and yet there they are attending conferences and seminars because they have an unquenchable thirst for knowledge to acquire or maintain the best advantage for their team and athletes in competition.

It is indeed easy and tempting to think, "I am just coaching my son's lacrosse team. I know enough to give them a good experience." In the course of a busy day of work, paying bills, transporting children and meal preparation these thoughts are understandable. However, that feeling of self-consolation we may give ourselves pales badly in the face of that awful feeling one gets when an athlete gives 100% and follows your instructions to the letter and then loses because you gave them inadequate advice.

It is hard to know where you need to expand your knowledge, especially when there is so much misinformation from so many sources in this age of the internet. Talking with respected coaches and finding a mentor are both excellent starts. Though initially pride or social shyness may get in the way of discussing training and strategy with others, know that it is a sign of strength to learn from fellow coaches. Great coaches may not share their playbook, but they are generally quite willing to share their knowledge if it will benefit an athlete, regardless of whether the athlete is on their team.

As an example of just how much there is to know as a coach, let's look at just one aspect of coaching, the strength and conditioning of the athlete. No sport functions at its best without a strength and conditioning program specific to the age group being coached. Today there is a Nationally Certified Strength and Conditioning Specialist program, and it has become more common, and is sometimes required, for colleges to have certified coaches on staff. It is less common for junior high or high schools to have CSCS specialists and extremely uncommon for a town league. This means that the coach typically is on his or her own in properly developing the athletes for their charge. (To appreciate what this means, look at the CSCS practice exam questions and areas of study on their website, cscs-questions.com.)

And this is just one area. You might want to review the visual eye tracking research in baseball or the probability statistics in basketball of who shoots best in what locations at what point in the game. Or how about the inverted U curve in athlete motivation? The things to know are expansive, from the tried-and-true fundamentals to the ever-evolving techniques and analytics. As the old saying goes, the more we learn the more we recognize how little we know. We owe it to all our athletes to be committed lifelong learners about their physiology and motivation, as well as the particulars of our sport. It keeps them safer and increases their chances of success. And of course, learning new ideas keeps coaching fresh and enjoyable each season.

THE COACH AS INSTRUCTOR

It would be so nice to bring our athletes into a classroom and lecture to them knowing they are riveted to every word and will fully know how to execute our instructions. It would be nice.

Our athletes learn in different modalities and do so differently at different stages of development in their capacity to learn. By "modalities" I mean cognitive, emotional, behavioral (including reflex) and social. Also, some individuals are more visual learners than auditory and some can visualize a schematic of a defense plan while others need practice, practice, practice, and to observe fellow teammates execute the play. Furthermore, some can learn proprioceptive movement simply by observing. For example, to teach me a country-western dance movement sequence by facing me requires me to observe it visually and reverse the movement in my mind, then execute it physically. While for me this is very difficult, for others it appears easy. More about this in a later chapter.

If you'd ever seen me try to dance, you would know it is important when instructing athletes to be sensitive to their modalities and learning styles. And your empathy for your athletes will increase if you spend some time thinking about how they individually learn and process information. Some instruction occurs in a designated format—like a classroom or on the court; some occurs individually with a pre-planned protocol based on an individual athlete's need; and some occurs spontaneously based on a coach's observation and athlete's readiness to learn.

Just how does a coach know when an athlete is ready to learn? The simplest answer is to know the athlete and help the athlete know you so they are comfortable asking questions. They need to know your philosophy and practice style in coaching and you need to know why they are interested in the sport and what sustains their interest. You also need to know their background and history in the sport. Without this information you are compromising the team's chance of success.

While there are different approaches to teaching, the *whole, part, whole* is the preferred approach. Here you have the athlete demonstrate the whole process of, for example, swinging a bat. Next, for the young athlete, give feedback about one or two things they are doing well (for example, "Your stance is good and you are keeping your eyes on the ball."), then one thing the athlete could change ("We will now show you how to use your core strength to have a powerful hit."). Following instruction of parts, the whole is once again practiced and feedback can continue. Some learn quickly and some take considerable time, but regardless of talent, all the necessary improvements never happen in one session, and sometimes not even in one season.

As a separate example, consider the football tight end who is learning the 100-meter dash. In demonstrating the whole, many young football players come out of the blocks with wide steps. It is as if they are about to be tackled (that would put a whole new twist on the hundred-meter dash). Feedback and instruction on accelerating out of the blocks involves explanation, marker setting and, at times, cell phone video feedback. The athlete then practices eliminating sidestepping out of the blocks. On another day you work with correcting the 'popping up' out of the blocks. To simply run a videotape and tell them all the errors overwhelms the athlete, generates frustration and does not allow the body to practice each part. To offer specific, constructive instruction in front of teammates can be a productive teaching tool for everyone, but it might also be very embarrassing and, depending on the individual and the circumstance, can shame the athlete. Shaming the athlete is never a productive teaching tool. As for when it is best to offer feedback in front of the other athletes or privately, this is a judgment call based on your best sense of what you think will be most effective for the athlete and the team.

Second, there continues to be value in the very old approach found in medical school teaching programs which is *see one, do one, teach one*. This worked well when I ran summer camps and had college student athletes teach junior high and high school students. I have also used it with senior athletes working with freshmen athletes.

One simple example is leading in warm-up plyometrics. I strongly recommend to listen carefully as your athletes "teach one" to another. Here you have the opportunity to hear and see how they conceptualized your work and how they provide feedback of technique or teaching style. Are they critical? Do they reinforce verbally? This may be a reflection of your teaching style. Done well, this enhances team bonding as well as learning for both athlete and coach. In addition, many of our athletes go on to become coaches and it is good to know how they are incorporating learning and teaching into their personal style.

The third approach is described by Bandura (1977) as "Component processes governing observational learning." Fundamentally it involves: *attention, retention, motor reproduction and reinforcement.*

Attention. With a young athlete, attention is limited. So, in this approach you begin by modeling or having the desired behavior modeled for the athlete. Modeling competent behavior is primary in reproducing subsequent learned behavior. For some, observational learning of modeled behavior is sufficient to produce the desired response. For others, feedback on the demonstrated behavior is necessary for coordinated motor learning to be established with the athlete.

Also, young athletes (as with most of us) will have many thoughts competing with your demonstration. Some examples include: "I'd better learn this or coach won't play me," or "I know teammate Tyler will pick on me if I don't get this right, and my arm is sore already," or "Is practice almost over because I am meeting the love of my 13-year-old life as soon as practice is done." Therefore, it is important to discern the learning interest level, the complexity of the task, the sensory component and the likely engagement.

Retention. This is where the athletes can cognitively organize the information in their heads and can then translate it from their minds to coordinated muscle activity. The athlete symbolically rehearses the activity and cognitively organizes it into the sequence they intend to perform.

Motor reproduction response. Here the athlete demonstrates the response based on his or her physical capabilities. Just as there are academic students who study a subject in school and recall without much effort, there are others who need to review, repeat and rehearse their subject. So also are athlete differences in the learning and practice time needed for success in learning new skills. Feedback is provided by the coach's verbal feedback and/or video self-observation with feedback. The motivated athlete will persevere to the target learning criteria.

Reinforcement. It is very important to find the motivational resources for each athlete. The young athlete generally requires external reinforcement in a tangible form, which could be as simple as a "Well done," or "We have worked hard today, let's pick it up tomorrow, who wants pizza? Tonight, think about what we practiced and we will continue tomorrow." Reinforcement needs to be tied closely in time to the behavior being reinforced.

However, for a college senior who is nationally competitive, the reinforcement is often more internal than external. The external continues to be necessary and important, but the internal is not to be underestimated. Indeed, if you believe the athlete is happy with their performance (self-reinforcement) and yet the athlete actually has a negative view of their performance, this could have an adverse effect on future performance. It is important to ask the athlete how he or she evaluates their performance and listen to not just their words but also the nonverbal expressions and tone of voice.

A third type of reinforcement is vicarious reinforcement. For an adolescent to see a professional basketball game where the winning shot is based on a fake pass followed by a fall away shot will leave the young basketball player practicing it in their head (vicarious reinforcement resulting in modeled behavior). If the coach did not see the same game he or she may wonder why three of his athletes are attempting to demonstrate that shot in practice.

Never underestimate the power of vicarious reinforcement whether it be positive or negative. Did you ever see a person observe someone getting a speeding ticket on the highway and the next day you check your speed as you approach that same location? This is an example of negative vicarious reinforcement that increases the likelihood of your being a good driving citizen, at least at that location.

If the reinforcement is sufficient, the athlete will be motivated to repeat the cycle of *attention, retention, motor reproduction* and *reinforcement*. Now if you couple this with the *whole, part, whole* method you have an excellent teaching tool. Then to see first-hand how your athletes are cognitively processing the information utilize the *see one, do one, teach one* approach.

Remember, it is important to understand you have little control over how individuals or groups are processing your information. You may want to be teaching based on videotaped feedback of errors made during a game. This can be very productive when the team individuals have a good sense of self-competency and embrace corrective feedback, but as noted above, it can also be quite negative. Imagine Maura making a mistake on a play and thinking, "Oh great, now coach is going to bring this up in practice in front of my teammates." From that point on, Maura may be thinking of the coach more than the play and become about one second behind the game, which is more than enough time to make more errors.

One strategy to assist in improving performance is, at the end of the game, as noted previously, have your athletes make notes in their journal (which they share with you) regarding what worked for them during the game and what they would have liked to have done differently. If Maura does not mention the errors, she may not know or may be embarrassed. Either way, it assists you in knowing how to work on an individual level with her as well as on a group level with the team. The latter is to discuss what went well and what can be improved. I have found in life, we often learn better from our errors than our successes. But young athletes need to hear about both where they succeeded and where they came up short.

In summary, the *whole, part, whole* method has demonstrated success in instruction whether teaching statistics or videotaped team feedback. With this as an overall foundation, Bandura's approach to learning via observational learning is foundational to any learning process. And finally, the *see one, do one teach one* provides the coach with excellent feedback on how well learning is occurring on the team and where gaps in learning may require the coach's attention.

SOCIAL, BEHAVIORAL, COGNITIVE LEARNING THEORY

In addition to the broad methodological perspective, there are a couple specific areas of psychology that are fundamental to understanding the athlete's learning. These include areas such as attribution, dissonance, behavioral conditioning, reflex learning and phenomenology.

The old school of learning assumes and relies upon a fairly linear process. Information is communicated to our senses where sensory coding occurs and there is a very short sensory memory. For example, you say, "Maddy, did you hear me?" whereupon she pauses then answers as if she heard when in fact she was not paying attention, and then when you asked if she heard, her attention was required and she processed auditory memory (listened to the request and provided the expected response).

Distraction had limited her attention, which may cause a coach to respond in frustration and punish the athlete —"Maddy, take a lap on the track!"—or ask what was distracting her. Next is short term memory, lasting just long enough to execute an activity such as "Soup is in aisle 3 about half way down on the left." This is followed by long term memory which requires verbal or visual rehearsal and strategies for remembering the intended item or event, such as memorizing the play book.

However, memory is more than that. We actually don't see the world directly. We see it through our memory. You don't have to look at an oval with 8 lanes surrounding a football field and wonder what it is; it comes to consciousness equipped with substance and meaning: it is a track where people run in a counterclockwise direction. *What you see is structured through your memory and passes through emotional centers of your brain and is presented with meaning and emotion as it comes to consciousness.* For example, one athlete sees a track and is motivated to do 800-meter repeats. Another sees a track and immediately becomes nauseous. What they see has passed through their brain's emotional center's history of memories as they come to conscious awareness of what they are observing. Each athlete's processing results in a slightly different experience.

This structuring of meaning of our environment prior to it being presented to consciousness is so fundamental, and yet most of us do not realize it is occurring within us. For example, we live in a carpentered society where most of what we see in our cities is vertical, horizontal and 90-degree angles. Many ancient tribes historically did not grow in a carpentered society. If you present a haystack it looks the same to both groups; however, if you ask each to find a needle in the haystack, the tribal member is far better equipped perceptually to find the needle that is neither in a vertical or horizontal position.

Even within a common community, we all see and experience the world quite differently from each other. For example, in my first year of coaching cross country all training was done in the athlete's regular running shoes as racing flats can incur injury if worn too often. Preparation for the first meet was thorough (so I thought). We discussed it all, including the emotional fever of going off the start line too fast. However, with all the preparation, on race day I noted a young freshman putting on his high school racing flats, using his key to adjust his spikes and his eyes were wide with anticipation. The sight of his racing shoes was a visual cue associated with race day memories, and therefore came complete with considerable emotions which overshadowed my instructions. I knew he would go off the line too fast. Indeed, we both learned much that first race day.

Given that when we look at the world, we do not see it directly, but rather, we see it through our memory, including both perceptual and emotional memory, it is incumbent on us to ask our athletes, "What does this mean to you?" The coach may think, with one minute left in this game, Talia has made this shot from ten feet 100 times before, but Talia tightens her shoulders with the uninvited gut sense that she has been here before where in the last minute she did not do well. Her response may not even be a verbal memory, just an emotional sensation. With her tightened shoulders, she throws up a brick resulting in an air ball and further conditioning her to miss in the final minute of future games.

This is where coach as guide/teacher can come in and use Bandura's approach to have Talia reflect with her coach's assistance and then proceed with a deconditioning or counter-conditioning program to manage the final minute anxiety in games.

Next, attribution theory can help with understanding athletes. What is important here is attributions are used to explain behavior. In general, we tend to explain other people's behavior as enduring characteristics of the person and our own behavior as temporary or changeable often due to environmental circumstances. For example, we see someone staggering out of a bar and we attribute their behavior to being an alcoholic, whereas if we were to stagger out from a bar it would be because it was a hard day, or a rainy day, or I was with a friend I have not seen in years.

An example of attribution in sports is that of a tennis player who has her best match ever and attributes her behavior to being prepared, but also to incredibly good fortune which may not be repeated (of course she keeps this to herself). Her competition is likely to believe this was a better player and her characteristic play is always that good or better. This is where the value of the coach comes into play. A coach may help cognitively restructure the win. It is restructured by the coach as a result of progressive improvement in performance due to her improved technique, practice, and concentration. The opposing coach needs to show their athlete how athletes have on and off days and make the case that if their athlete continues to improve she will be in a good position to capture the next match.

Classical conditioning is reflex learning. For example, you don't recognize your dehydration and at the 4k mark of a 5k race you feel light-headed and don't complete the race. After finding nothing on medical workup you are informed you were likely dehydrated. However, at the next meet on the 4k mark you feel light-headed once again and reduce your speed to the finish line even though this time you were properly hydrated. If not metabolic, this may be a conditioned response and consulting with a sports psychologist would be valuable to the athlete. Pre-competition anxiety is a classically conditioned response to the environment, resulting in one feeling nauseous or having the need to urinate, or other conditioned reactions. Moderate anxiety is good. However, it can be classically conditioned to stimulate increased physiological activity which the athlete may not notice and which may result in poor performance. Classical conditioning can tie race day anxiety to lack of appetite and proper hydration. Check out the Port-O-Let use by athletes prior to the start of a marathon and you will notice some good hydration being lost to conditioned anxiety resulting in increased urinary output.

Operant condition is based on the action of a person in the environment. It works well with Bandura's approach discussed above. A foundational example of this is reward and punishment. Punishment does not eliminate a behavior; it inhibits it while the threat is present. For example, a coach who uses punishment as a strategy is out sick and the team therefore relaxes the workout as there are no punishing consequences for that day

When reinforcing a behavior, it is important, in the beginning, to reinforce it on every occasion, then reduce the frequency of reinforcement as the athlete progresses. Based on the above, the new athlete needs external reinforcement, which becomes less important over time as the athlete learns to internally reinforce him or herself. With that said, talk with Olympic coaches and you will see some reinforcement is always needed.

Reinforcement must be closely associated in time to the desired behavior and must be seen as reinforcement by the athlete. Again, this means the coach needs to get to know the athlete. For example, it does not benefit your athlete to provide the reward of pizza on Friday for a behavior today unless there is the verbal reinforcement of a promise of forthcoming pizza or reward. This promise is called a secondary reinforcer. I always ask new team members what they like and dislike about the sport and what they prefer from their coach if they have a bad day. For example, do they do best with some space after the event or do they do best with immediate feedback.

Team culture is a powerful source of team reinforcement. Here is where the relationship with your captains is critical to the program. For example, your weakest athlete underperforms and you criticize him in front of the team not knowing he just got news that his grandfather has died. Further, you did not know he is best friends with your star athlete who underperforms at the next meet in part because he harbors a grudge against you as coach. A word from a captain coupled with support (reinforcement) in the form of, "Ryan, we are here for you and sorry for your loss," is critical to team culture. Also, this behavior is what we want to see for our developing youth.

The best time to teach is as close to the practice as possible, and if it is not an aerobically intense practice, the
brain is best able to learn after exercise, not before. The
rationale for this is discussed in the chapter on the brain.
Before practice, give only the rationale for the current work
and assignments. In designing the practice make the learning outcomes realistic. If you aren't sure what that means
look at the following numbers for 10 seconds: 2 4 3 7 4 1 5
9 and then turn away for 30 seconds. Now try to recite all
the numbers in reverse order and you will know how many
an overwhelmed athlete feels. The point is, keep the session
to key points, tell them what you are going to tell them,
tell them, then give them a summary of what they need to
remember (the "take-aways"). This is especially important
when discussing strategy or play book.

BRINGING IT ALL TOGETHER

As a coach, it is important to know how your athlete
experiences the world through their memory and experience. They are not fully aware of how they structure their
world through their memory, which includes gender, culture, race, as well as a myriad of personal qualities. Get
to know the athlete and be able to ask, "What does this
mean to you?" This question is best done after you have
a coach/athlete relationship. Do it directly or through
journals or such.

Know that athletes may attribute an error or success to
personal situational circumstances, and you—not being
them—are more likely to attribute the behavior to enduring
traits or patterns of behavior. Again, listen to the athlete as
a preface to educating the athlete.

Bandura's approach to conditioning is a valuable addition to *see one, do one, teach one* and *whole, part, whole* teaching methods. Also, reinforcement has to be immediate and valued by the athlete. For the new athlete, reinforcement must be external and clear: "Good job, Matt, you squared your shoulders; now let's work on the positioning of your hands." (Positive first, then an improvement recommendation.)

When it comes to reflex learning behavior, such as the unintentional conditioning of an anxiety response to game day racing flats, it becomes important to acknowledge the response. Also, to use *in vivo* (in life) practice during non-game days to decondition the anxiety producing relationship. For example, short practice sessions with the racing flats on and positive self-statements established with the coach.

Considering the time and effort the above approaches require, you may find yourself thinking, "Sheesh, I'm a coach, not a psychologist." You would not be the first one to feel this way, and it usually happens with a particular athlete or group of athletes amidst the challenges of a season. While it may help at many times in coaching to be a psychologist that is not the point. What matters is that as a teacher/guide you take the time and care and to know the athletes for whom you are responsible. Knowing them and understanding in some way how they are experiencing the preparation and competition will help them, will help you, and will most definitely help the team to succeed. An appreciation of these learning strategies, and which best fit the athlete at a given time, further enhances the likelihood of success.

FIVE

COMMUNICATION, COACH AND PARENT

I n any sport there are all the non-rostered members of a team whom the coach cannot cut and with whom he or she must have a positive relationship if they are to help the adolescent and also make progress towards winning. These members have a major influence on the outcome of both the game and the joy of being involved in the sport. They are the parents, the bus driver, the athletic director, the school nurse, the guidance counselor, the teachers, the trainer, the principal, and the media. These people neither score the winning point nor defend against losing a game, meet or match. However, they can provide wonderful assistance and support and are very much part of a coach's responsibility. It is the most important non-rostered members of the team who are the focus of this chapter, specifically parents.

As a coach, you will typically find parents of athletes to be either a valuable member of the team, or a significant challenge to your joy as coach; or in some cases you will not find them at all, as they are essentially invisible persons. To offer a few familiar examples, a parent can help with fundraising, transportation, team snacks, cheerleading, supporting their child's fellow team members, reinforcing rules and being a support to the child when they experience defeat and don't want to return to the team.

Of course, a parent can also offer criticism when uninvited—especially during a game or meet. The parent can pose an emotional threat to the coach's sense of self-worth and control of team integrity. When one considers the already significant tasks of paperwork, scheduling and attending to the myriad of details while trying to put into practice the principles described in these chapters, adding on a tug of war with a parent can make coaching an onerous chore and a truly unpleasant experience.

Poor parent behavior in youth sports is unfortunately stereotypical in its familiarity, such that examples of horror stories populate the internet. One site, for example, documents horror stories from high school coaches.[2] A few examples are all that's needed to provide an all too familiar picture of worst-case scenarios:

"My starting quarterback decided to cut two classes (one of them was mine). I confronted him about this and he stated that he went home to get an assignment that was due. I checked with the teacher and found out it wasn't true. I informed the young man that he would be benched for the first half of the upcoming game. This did not go over well with the parents. After calling me just about every name in the book, they went to the administration and had my decision reversed. I was let go after the season."

"A group of parents went door-to-door of current and former players literally asking if they had any "dirt" on me in hopes of getting rid of me."

2.   https://www.syracuse.com/highschoolsports/article/in-their-own-words-high-school-coaches-tell-their-horror-stories/

"I had a parent call me at 11 p.m. after we had won a sectional semifinal game. He was angry because I didn't have his child run the play that won us the game."

On another site, coaches reveal some of their worst experiences.[3] In one a player quit while his dad was out of town. When his dad returned he was told that his son was cut from the team, so he tried unsuccessfully to sue the coach and the school. In another a coach was sued over a yearbook picture when a kid quit before the end of the season.

You could spend hours finding similar anecdotes about nightmare experiences coaches have had and hear still more war stories from current and former coaches, but I don't recommend this as a good use of your time. Interestingly, while the internet can provide many examples of what a parent should and should not do, there are very few examples of positive parent behavior, and it isn't easy to find examples of parent behaviors which coaches actually cherished. Yet, after years of coaching, I have developed many wonderful relationships with parents of our college athletes and my wife and I have been to many weddings of their children. And I know my experiences are not unique, but rather a common experience for many coaches.

So, as you seek out guidance and mentorship from other coaches, instead of prodding them to gossip about their worst experiences with parents, prompt them to tell you about their positive experiences and impacts they have had with the families of their athletes. You will be encouraged and likely surprised by some of the things you hear.

Meanwhile, of course, you do need to be able to manage the inevitable conflicts. In any enterprise where families are

3. https://www.al.com/highschoolsports/article/problems-with-parents-coaches-reveal-their-worst-experiences/

invested in their children and where competition is at the center of the activity, some conflict is inevitable. Keep in mind that in the vast majority of these cases the conflict is present because the parents deeply love and care for their children and, like all of us, want the best for them. They are trying to guide a child through adolescence and the angst and difficulty of that is bound to spill over into activities like sports.

As a psychologist, I have mediated many disputes, and while on occasion, there may be a challenging personality disorder involved in the mix, it is most often a problem of weak and confused communication of expectations. As you try to navigate the many aspects of coaching your athletes, you don't need an angry parent calling a school board member around budget time who then calls the principal who calls the athletic director who is worried about budget approval, and on it goes in a swirl that will inevitably be escalated by the flurry of social media posts. While you are not immune to such scenarios and there is no guarantee you won't accumulate some horror stories of your own, you may decrease that likelihood by following these two recommendations: 1) Establish and maintain clear communication and expectations from the very beginning and 2) Never go it alone as a coach.

Schools and city leagues have rules defining relationships. Also, there are state and federal laws which must be complied with and understood. For example, before you coach a minor, you need to complete a police background check. So, while major issues with parents can be mitigated by clear municipal and state laws and school and league regulations, my focus here is on the relationship issues that have nothing to do with institutionally established rules and laws.

For example, immediately after a game a parent says, "My child has been to every practice and has dreams of being a goalie and yet you never give her a chance. What is wrong with you?" If you have a preseason agreement stating game strategy will not be discussed immediately following a game this is to your advantage. To be able to say, "I will review this with our assistant coach and we will discuss it at our meeting on Tuesday," will allow the parent time to calm down and then have a reasonable and hopefully productive discussion. This also gives you time to review the matter with your assistant coach and gain another perspective. If you don't have an assistant coach please follow my second piece of advice about not going it alone—and find one!

Parent preparation for the season: In order to make your journey in coaching more enjoyable and maximize your work with parents, there needs to be clearly negotiated guidelines for your relationship with the athletes and parents in advance of preseason. Also, there needs to be a clear understanding of consequences when the relationship contract is broken as well as avenues for appeal of the coach's decision when a rule is broken by a parent or athlete. While junior high, high school and city leagues will recommend preseason meetings, meetings are often bypassed in the excitement of starting preseason. This is a serious mistake. As difficult as the horror story scenarios above are, each of them would be much easier to resolve if there were clearly defined rules and boundaries agreed to and signed at the start of the season. Such agreements need to involve not just the athletes and the parents, but the athletic director.

In expounding upon my advice to "Never go it alone" I wish to say a few specific things about the relationship of the coach to the athletic or program director. Whether coaching a town league or working in a school system, it is important to appreciate the multiple roles administrators must play in their jobs. While there are now degree programs in sports administration, it is still more usual to expect an administrator to be someone who had to "come through the ranks" and has completed on-the-job learning of their administrative role.

An administrator manages two types of teams, the flagship sports teams that draw significant public interest and the other ships. You know if you are flagship or other ship. For the "other ships" generally the administrator desires the student athlete to have a good developmental growth experience, and be a team that stays within budget and does not embarrass the department or school. In today's litigious environment, a coach often is readily sacrificed when conflict emerges. There are many instances of when a coach's behavior is questioned such that when a complaint emerges a posture of protecting the youth and the program becomes a primary focus of the administrator. Unfortunately, it can be the opposite of innocent until proven guilty.

A coach cannot live in fear or apprehension of a false allegation, but can take steps to minimize likelihood of its occurrence and then get on with enjoying the journey of guiding the young athlete's development. One of those steps is to have a transparent and trusting relationship with the person overseeing the program, and to meet with that person regularly, sharing any concerns. The last thing an administrator wants is a surprise, and regular communication goes a long way towards preventing surprises. Everything I say in this chapter about the relationship with parents applies as well to the person overseeing your work. Do all you can to make sure that in victory or defeat, conflict or harmony, you are not alone.

As for parental agreements, I know many coaches, and there are many internet examples of parents agreeing to read and sign a contract regarding expectations and responsibilities for the season of competition. Such agreements are best treated as contracts negotiated with the team within established rules and laws. But we also need to recognize the limits of such agreements. To begin with, legally binding contracts are typically the result of negotiation, and given that the parent has little bargaining power, many parents sign the agreement as a means to an end and are not really sold on the contract's role on their youth's team.

So, while such contracts can be a good idea, they are only a first step. The following recommendations are next steps that can greatly reduce stress during the season.

First, in addition to clearly establishing the coach's expectations of athletes and parents, have parents articulate their own expectations. Invite them to write what they hope their child will ideally accomplish during the course of the season and what they can reasonably expect their child to accomplish. You can organize these expectations into categories of social development, skill level, and so on. Ask them to note if they discussed these expectations with their child. These written expectations offer you the opportunity to assess whether the athletes' and parents' expectations are realistic and discuss what happens if the goals they seek are not attainable given available resources and time. You may also counsel the parent in advance for planned alternatives if, for example, the team is too big for their child to get the attention the parents desire for them.

As an example, a large football squad has an incredible amount of work to do to have a unified team that can execute plays. There may be limited time to work with a youngster on strength and flexibility to improve acceleration off the line or cutting techniques on the field. It may be recommended that the athlete and their parents find a certified a strength and conditioning coach if one is not available at your school.

If you are coaching athletes under 18, it is recommended you write the rules and have them sign along with their parents. While a minor's signature generally has no legal weight, it has the value of reinforcing character development. Perhaps equally important, you have the parent complete a questionnaire as you would your athletes. Following their answers, the parent then signs the commitment. The parent gives consent and the child gives assent. Here are some examples of important questions you may want parents to consider:

- What would you like your child to gain from participation this season?

- What do you see as your child's strengths as an athlete?

- What do you see as your child's weaknesses as an athlete?

- What do you see as the best possible outcome for your child this season?

- What do you see as an average outcome for your child this season?

- What can you, as a parent, offer to best support your team this season? (If they don't know, let them say "I don't know" and consider that an invitation for you to contact them. Also, you can list items such as snacks, equipment, transportation, etc.)

- What is the best way to communicate with you? (phone, email, biweekly meetings)

After parents have responded to these questions the next step is for you to review each of the parents' goals and hopes for the season and select those where you see a clear conflict with your plans, abilities or resources. Openly acknowledging your limitations as well as the limitations of the program establishes an important boundary. As noted above, you need to clearly communicate these limitations with the parent before the start of the season. If the parent insists on their child's involvement and you agree, you document the conversation and leave it on file. This is invaluable should the future bring an unfortunate accusation by the parent that you did not properly prepare their child.

There are internet examples off parent agreements that may precede the more open-ended questions to which parents are asked to respond: One specific example is the Jones Middle School Athletics Parent Contract.[4]

Having parents complete questionnaires and agreements like the ones described above gives the coach insight into where concerns may emerge and provides the opportunity to intervene preemptively before a problem develops with a parent. Also, as noted above, the athletic or league director needs to be fully aware of plans and agreements.

4. (https://www.boone.k12.ky.us/userfiles/1304/my%20files/athletics/parent%20contract%206-13.pdf?id=450068)

Written agreements and proactive conversations that clearly establish common expectations are crucially important to avoiding future conflicts. But some conflict is inevitable, so I want to offer some insights in this regard. First, and I know this is difficult advice to follow, but *never show anger.* Anger is a sign of a one-down position and usually results in a defensive posture by the other person. It is perfectly natural and okay to feel the frustration and want to express anger or seek avoidance when a parent expresses anger or frustration. But it is important to maintain a calm demeanor. Anger indicates loss of control.

We all have memories of our youth based on emotional experiences. For example, a parent may admonish you not to run in the street. To this day as you head toward the street to retrieve a ball a voice in your head says, "Stop, look both ways." That is the voice of the parent within, developed and engrained over many years. It can attempt to control, as in keeping you from being hit by a car, or it can be nurturing such as, "I was up all night with my sick baby and have to go to work. I am tired, but I would have it no other way—nice job."

In its simple form, there is the parent within us who punishes or rewards us. Psychologist Eric Berne cautions us that when we use or hear such terms as should, must, ought to, have to, got to, this reflects a controlling internal parent. While there is a time for such parenting, it generally controls and does not develop the young athlete. To say, "You should only steal second base on my signal," is different from saying, "You should be ashamed of yourself for not watching for my signal. You let the entire team down."

Examples of statements to coaches that may elicit negative feelings include the following:

1. "Coach, you <u>should</u> play Mary in Lacrosse as she wants to be with her friends."

2. "Coach, you <u>must</u> be off the field by 4:30. If you have a problem, see the athletic director."

3. "Coach, our daughter is a really good player. You <u>ought</u> to buy her the hockey sticks."

4. "Coach, you <u>have to</u> tell me now why my Yolanda was benched today. You know she is better than your daughter!"

These are parenting statements that easily bring out the frustration or anger in us. When you say things to yourself such as, "I don't get paid enough," or, "The athletic director likes field hockey more than us," or, "This team would be more fun if this parent would go away and leave us alone," you are expressing normal human emotions drawn from the emotions within (limbic structures of the brain). The sooner you recognize that these feelings are facilitated by parental statements by others, the better prepared you will be to respond adult to adult rather than child to parent.

For example, immediately after a game a parent says, "You are a terrible coach!" You want to say, "Hey, fella, this is my first year and I did it because no one else would. I'm doing the best I can and your son is not going to be scouted anyhow." But it will be much more productive to be aware the parent's feelings and set boundaries to it with, "Let's talk tomorrow after practice as we agreed not to talk immediately after a game." Note that your tone of voice in making this statement will be very important in setting a tone for the meeting. Tomorrow the parent may be calm or may continue with a negative emotional style of communication. Don't go it alone, have your assistant with you to facilitate the meeting and as a witness to the parent's stated needs. The next chapter revisits this communication strategy for the athletes.

Next, you invoke the equivalent of the famous words of President Kennedy's inauguration address. Instead of asking the parent what the team can do for them and their child, you ask the parent how they can best assist the team. Asking someone to work may get parental involvement, but more often it gets something just as helpful. It silences the critics.

While reading this you may think, "That is not what I would do but I don't know what to do." This is why a good mentor is worth their weight in gold. Look to a retired coach in your community who impressed you as a coach and whose personality you find accommodating to your personality. Invite the coach to coffee and discussion. You may be impressed with how readily they will assist you in avoiding pitfalls and obstacles as well as offering tips and strategies not found in the literature. My mentor, retired coach George Davis, was that person for me. After a year of conversations, in gratitude I asked him about his generosity, to which he replied, "I do it for the athletes."

In summary: Have a preseason meeting and learn parent expectations. Establish with them that their child's athletic activity is a partnership and a relationship. Negotiate expectations and ascertain where expectations may be beyond what can be offered. Never go it alone! Have an assistant coach who can support the athletes by diffusing relationship issues which will emerge and help with game play. Have an open and clear relationship with your athletic or program director and make sure you communicate what you are doing (especially any written agreements) with her or him. Finally, know that any expression of anger or avoidance of emotional confrontation with parents is ultimately a recipe for disaster. Be prepared for difficult conversations. Listen and do whatever it takes to remain calm in those exchanges. People will inevitably have complaints in the course of a season, but they will be appreciative if the coach can be relied on to be the calm and steady one amidst the feverish emotions of competition.

SIX

ATHLETE/COACH COMMUNICATION AND GOAL SETTING

This chapter combines two seemingly different areas, which at first may appear an odd coupling. While guidance on specific sport goal development can be found in many places on the internet, goals alone cannot drive a winning recipe. The goals have to be communicated between the athlete and coach and communication occurs on many levels, as does, alas, miscommunication. Effective communication involves structured thoughts, feelings and emotions expressed both behaviorally and verbally in a relational context of two or more people. As a prologue to a discussion of thoughtful and effective goal-setting, therefore, it seems to me imperative that we first treat the many aspects of communication necessary to understand the athlete in relation to the coach. Only successful communication between coach and athlete will generate the necessary buy-in to goals and the accompanying motivation to pursue the goals.

Further, as will be seen, goals are complex and vary based on type, season and individual strengths and weaknesses. To establish effective communication and lay a foundation for goals that produce desired results is indeed a very challenging task. The complexity of this task further reinforces what was said in the second chapter: the successful coach understands that the devil (as well as the angel) is in the details.

THE WIN AND COMMUNICATION

We enter into coaching a sport with a desire to win the big game and to influence the lives of our young athletes. While losing a game, meet or match certainly can teach us more than a win, I have rarely seen a coach enter a game with the desire to lose. The rare exception was a coach from another team, who, midway through a game and early in the season, believed the athletes would do well to lose. Presumably this was to use the loss to challenge the athletes and engage a further bonding influence.

On that day, I observed this successful career coach confronting the referee and he seemed to ask to be tossed from the game. He was tossed by the ref, who appeared happy to oblige him. His collegiate athletes would later say that following the loss, their coach had some very intense workouts and presented with a stern attitude that helped unite the team. This strategy is not recommended for junior high and rarely, if ever, for high school.

Winning and losing a game has strong implications for both the individual and the team. It is my experience that when the athlete wins, they don't need their coach and are happy to be with teammates and family. There is a post-game brief review then perhaps discussion later in the week at a team meeting. However, when a team loses this is a valuable time to check in with both the team and individual athletes.

As noted in a previous chapter, this is where negative self-talk can solidify a negative attitude when a young athlete says, "They scored against me, I am too slow." The coach can assist to shift a negative cognition with something like, "We will work on speed and reaction time; also I think you were looking at their face not their body, we will work with it. See you Monday at practice." Here the athlete does not lie in bed self-loathing and thinking, "Coach thinks I am stupid and slow and I know Bill wants my position." Rather it is more likely for the athlete to think, "Bill wants my position and I hate that I missed the kick, but I want to know how coach will help me get faster."

This may not work with all athletes but it is far better than leaving them with their negative thoughts. We definitely cannot know what an athlete is doing or how they are interpreting their activities unless we ask them. As I have already noted, I typically ask at the start of the season how the athlete prefers their coach to respond to a defeat. Timing is critical in all important communication, and especially when offering corrective feedback to an athlete who made an error resulting in game loss.

As examples of not knowing what athletes are thinking or feeling unless they are asked, I offer here two broad experiences of college athletes from two sports. On one team were NCAA recruited collegiate varsity athletes who worked hard and sought the win. To suggest they sit down and miss a practice segment would be met with frustration on their part. Indeed, athletes would occasionally hide a cold or minor injury out of fear of being taken out of practice or a meet. Following this experience, I agreed to take on the club track team as the varsity teams did not have an out-of-season varsity track experience. As there was no varsity track team, the club would compete against other varsity teams at sister colleges. As it was a college club and not a varsity sport, the club had no recruiting and no cuts. As such, it admitted students who competed in high school and wanted to play in college, as well as athletes who had no prior experience (many of them).

Soon the day came when, with planned practice distances and recovery times in hand, I was engaged in 800-meter practice with a group of club athletes. About ten minutes into practice I noticed a couple of athletes complaining about the workout. I gently said, "If you are tired go ahead and take a seat." These two athletes sat down and upon others noticing the rest break, all but a few, who were high school athletes, also took a seat. In that moment I realized I did not know my new team or their motivations, so I proceeded to put the same effort into knowing their goals and motives as I had done with the varsity team. In time, and with understanding of motivation and goals of the club members and team, we too had athletes who resisted leaving practice to relax.

One additional club team story is the senior football player who completed his football eligibility and asked if he could throw the javelin. It was late spring season and I told him it is a club sport and I would allow it, but the last meet was in a week and we were invited to participate at a DI university hosted meet. He decided to throw and on the day of the event was taking a nap in the bleachers up until about a half hour prior to the event. At that time he was awakened and proceeded to compete using a borrowed javelin. His first toss was aesthetically beautiful to watch and resulted in gaining him second place overall in the DI event. He then returned to his nap in the bleachers. This gentleman was a unique exception to what is being written here about communication in goal development.

The point is every team is as unique as the athletes on the team. A clear understanding of individual and team dynamics is fundamental to the development of goals. This is because goals are developed in a relational context of coach and athlete/team, requiring solid interpersonal communication. This communication includes the stated facts and negotiated contracts and recognition of the athlete's and the coach's emotional readiness to endorse goals based on reciprocal negotiation.

HOW WE COMMUNICATE

This was discussed previously and is expanded on here because the ability to understand coach and athlete relationships is as fundamental to the win as is an understanding of the game and game strategy. All communication is done in a relational context and includes cognitions, affect and behavior, or in other words: thinking, feeling and doing.

From the communication between two cells in the brain to communication in a socio-cultural-economic context, communication is incredibly complex. Hundreds of textbooks have been written on the subject of effective communication and webinars and symposia on the topic abound. For the purposes here, communication is discussed in the context of a late 1950's concept of communication as transactions. It is based on statements such as should, must, ought to, got to and have to which can set limits on behavior as well as induce occasional feelings of shame or guilt when we fall short of expectations.

Hopefully, there were also people in our lives who set wonderful phrases for building self-esteem and expectations such as, "I am proud of you" or "Good job." For many, these voices still lie within us. Also the primitive emotional feelings of our youth are easily aroused by cues in the environment. Just try grabbing a pointed stick without hearing a voice in your head saying, "Careful, you'll put your eye out with that!" is not easy as for most it is a highly conditioned memory.

The truth is we don't know the voices in our athletes' heads and we often don't recognize our own voices. I recall one recruiting trip I made to a large cross country racing event. I had some time and was watching athletes and coaches preparing for their event. A young athlete approached his coach and said, "Coach, why do we have to do [such and such]?" to which the coach, who did not appear pressed for time, replied, "Because I told you to," and the athlete sheepishly walked away. Perhaps the coach was assigned a coaching role as part of a teaching contract and did not know why they had to do "such and such"; perhaps it was an athlete who asked the coach a question once too often, resulting in impatience on the part of the coach. Whatever the reason, watching the young athlete walking away with shoulders drooped and head down did not seem to convey the formula for a winning season or for the development of the athlete.

While we all have memories that make up our "parent" voice, we also were all children at one time and experienced happy and sad emotions, many of which we did not understand. As adults, it is easy to trigger childhood emotions in us. We then attempt to deal with these emotions directly or temper them with reason and logic.

Sports provide a wonderful arena for, among other things, learning about our emotions and how to manage them. To see an opposing team member cheat is frustrating. To complain to the ref that this person is cheating and have the ref ignore the plea for justice is a powerful life learning experience. You can stomp your feet and walk off the field (saw this in T-ball once), or begin cheating yourself, knowing the ref may not notice (life lesson here), or you can compete harder and focus on the game. These are all part of learning about emotion management. Once again the coach is a teacher and therapist.

For a coach to say "You should be here on time" invokes whatever feelings an athlete has toward their parent, be it a thought of, "I won't be late because coach will be mad," or, "If I am late I am a bad person and I will feel bad." Alternatively, a coach could say, "Practice starts at 4:00. If you are late, you will be off the roster for the game this week." As adults, we can imagine these same scenarios related to our work and appreciate how a boss who says "You should" can raise emotions. For our boss to say, "I need the Johnson report by Tuesday as we are having a board meeting Tuesday night," is sufficient. But to add, "You should get this done for me," adds a statement that is more parent and does not generally facilitate productive emotions.

In addition to *parent* and *child* communication going on inside us in the process of communication is the "adult." The adult emerges as we learn to negotiate and reason in an ever-changing environment. In our own head the adult can temper the parent: "No I am not going to feel guilty. I have never cut class and this is senior day and I did get into Harvard." The adult can also temper the child: "Wow, these carnival onion rings look awesome, but I have a game in the morning so I will hold off."

The transactional component comes when two individuals need to communicate with each other. In any communication we bring to it our *parent, adult* and *child*. All three communicate (often in distinct nonverbal ways) with the other person's *parent, adult* and *child.* As will be discussed later, communication on the verbal level includes words and, in addition, inflection, tempo, pace and such, as well as nonverbal expressions. Here are some models of communication between coach and athlete, based on the theory of Thomas Harris, Ph.D., that indicate how complicated communication can be with other people. Note, winning seasons are premised on good coach/athlete communication within the context of coach/athlete personalities.

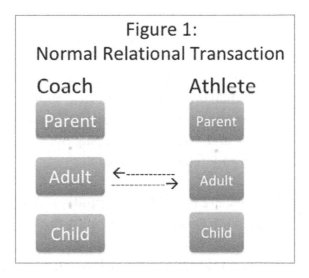

Here, in Figure 1, the transaction is logical and reasoned. For example,

Coach: "Practice is changed from 4:00 to 4:30 today."

Captain: "Thanks, coach, I will let the guys know." Or

Coach: "With this pitcher, you can take a bigger lead off first base."

Athlete: "Thanks, coach."

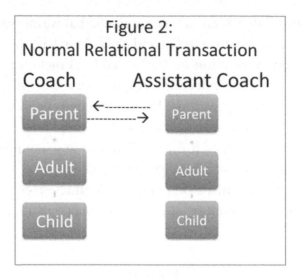

Figure 2:
Normal Relational Transaction
Coach   Assistant Coach

Parent ←-------- Parent
        -------→

Adult   Adult

Child   Child

Figure 2 presents a normal transaction which may occur between two parents, in this case, between a coach and her assistant. While it may not be the best approach, it is a common approach. Again, words such as 'should', 'must', 'ought to', 'got to' and 'have to' often bring out the child in the athlete being addressed by the coach.

For example:

Coach: "They are really dragging today. We ought to teach them a lesson. Let's have them run sprints."

Assistant coach: "Great idea, let's do it."

Coach to the athletes: "You are all looking pretty sloppy today; you should come ready to work out. We are going to do some suicide sprints and maybe next time you will come ready to work out."

The alternate adult to adult would be, "We all seem a bit tired today, let's get our heart rates up before we work out. We will do some gradual accelerations and will be ready." The end goal is the same; yet this is a very different approach and does not usually bring out the resistant child in the athlete. Later the coach may ask the captains about their perception of why the team appears fatigued. If the captain says, "Coach, they are in midterms," that is fine; or the captain may not know, but would have experienced the respect and inclusion of the coach.

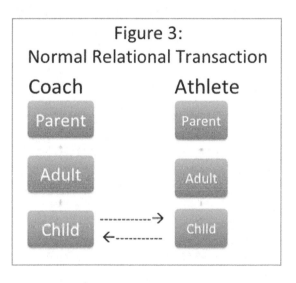

Figure 3:
Normal Relational Transaction

In this transaction we have the example of a coach who is proud of the team in their effort in the game. While thinking as an adult in terms of release, parent approval and such, the child in the coach says to the team, "I am proud of how you all worked so hard as a team today. You did everything exactly as practiced and for that I am taking our team out for pizza." The team responds, "Yippee!" While the transaction is child to child (it could be seen as a healthy parent to child interaction), the coach is aware of timing, effort, and even the young athlete who is sulking as this athlete did not feel their effort was good enough to merit pizza.

In this instance the coach sees the sulking and based on knowledge of the athlete knows it is more a characteristic of her/his typical behavior and says nothing. The bottom line is, even though the coach embraces the inner child, the coach is aware of effects on the team and, though acting as a child, the inner adult and parent continue to be vigilant. A positive outcome may be team bonding and a positive evaluation of their coach as holding clear standards that brought them the good team performance.

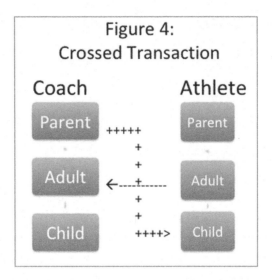

Crossed transactions can be problematic and lead to hurt feelings, decreased motivation and burnout. In this situation, the young athlete was delayed for practice due to a teacher consultation that had not been scheduled. While the athlete may have said, "Sorry I am late, coach, my teacher held me after class to talk about my report," the athlete simply says instead, "Sorry I am late, coach." This is clearly an attempt by the young athlete to have an adult interaction while at the same time feeling anxious about being late. Here the coach says as a parent to child, "Everyone else is here on time; you are letting your team down and you should consider your priorities—do six suicide runs on the field." Instead, coach could have said, "I don't understand as you are never late, let's meet for a few minutes after practice to clear things up." Note that besides the words expressed here, the tone of voice can imply a parental attitude that yields a crossed transaction.

In these situations, we all benefit from feedback from others. Here a good relationship with an assistant coach can be invaluable. Also, discussions with seasoned mentors as to how they manage these situations are a great asset in continued development as a coach. Remember, a winning season is founded on powerful sensitivity to details—and communication is no exception.

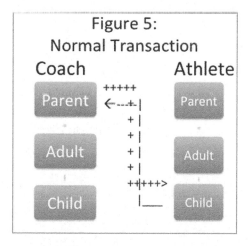

While this is a normal transaction it needs to be used carefully and seldom employed with your athletes. As an example, in a summer camp there was a young athlete who returned from a trail run proclaiming she had been stung by a bee. She had an allergy and was quite emotional about the sting. We brought her to the nursing staff who provided her with instructions on how to self-inject her epinephrine and the staff notified her parents. About 45 minutes later camp was ending and this 16 year old, newly licensed to drive, said goodbye to her counselor (a safety requirement to do prior to leaving camp).

On an adult to adult level I asked her if driving was a wise idea and she said her parents said it is okay. I then took on a parent attitude and said, "You have never taken epinephrine before and it is uncertain how your body is using it, so driving is not a good idea (she was acting like she was stimulated). I said, "If you get pulled over you will be charged with driving under the influence and that will be on your record, so how about calling your parents?" If she said no, we would have called her parents. By the way, her parents were appreciative and responded quite well to our request to pick her up.

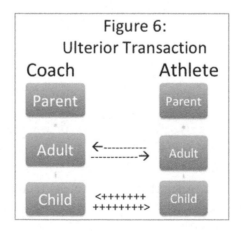

Figure 6:
Ulterior Transaction

THE HUMAN DIMENSION

This type of transaction is perhaps the most complex form of communication and often leads to misunderstanding and hurt feelings. Here you have a frustrated coach whose athlete is continuing to exhibit a bad habit. For example a baseball player whose ritual at the plate continues to leave him slow in initiating the swing of the bat. The frustrated coach approaches the player and instructs him as to his error, to which the player responds with "Thanks coach." This is an adult to adult interaction. However, here the coach's frustration is expressed in the form of clenched jaw, angry expression and voice louder than usual. The athlete's verbal response is fine; however the coach does not notice the athlete's tightening of his shoulders and overall increased tension which places the athlete in a poor position to succeed at the plate. The athlete says to a fellow player, "What's up with coach?" and the other player says, "Don't worry, he gets like that sometime. He just wants you to learn. He really cares." Or the other player says, "He gets mad a lot, you don't want to be on his list."

As humans we get frustrated, and frustration is normal. Young athletes learn how to negotiate in their developing world through navigating relationships with a human coach. It is important for the coach to invoke their *adult* and be able to say, usually at the end of practice, "I came down hard on you because I know you have potential and you really care..." something to that effect.

Of course there are times when a coach intentionally raises a voice, acts frustrated or angry to focus attention or draw a team together. Without some show of emotion, it is easy for a team to believe the coach does not care for them or the sport. A coach's passion is very important, but it must be intentional and, after the fact, reflected upon as to its success with the athletes. I have known college coaches to swear when an athlete fails a routine and I have known coaches to get silent (athletes find coach silence incredibly disconcerting and this may have a tactical value). For one coach to swear and the athlete to say, "It's ok, I know he cares," and for a different coach to swear and have an athlete say, "He is a real jerk," is significantly different. Usually, in one instance the coach is swearing at the behavior and in the other the coach is swearing at the athlete.

Demeaning a behavior is clearly different from demeaning a person. Note the difference in "That was such a dumb execution" and "You are so dumb." While I do not find literature supporting swearing as an effective tool in coaching, I am confident that demeaning the person is an ingredient in the recipe of a losing season.

In the Christian tradition there is a saying, "Hate the sin but love the sinner." A well-known psychologist, Carl Rogers, echoes this teaching that we should accept the person unconditionally but hold the person accountable for their behavior. To remove an athlete from the team for consistent rule violations, *while still respecting the person* can be a challenge, but it is fundamental to our role modeling for our young athletes.

Along these lines, I recall a situation years ago when, during preseason, our team agreed to a dry (alcohol-free) season and everyone signed on board with the decision. The second week, a new athlete was reported to have been drunk on a Saturday evening. I informed the athlete that per the agreement, there would be a loss of competition time and a second infraction would mean their decision to leave the team would be respected (as stated in the agreement). A second occurrence resulted in a meeting where

I informed the athlete the decision to leave the team is respected. As it turned out it was the parents who wanted the student to play sports in college whereas the student wanted the freedom to make his own choices in college. In this case the *parent* voice was quite literally what brought the athlete to the team. The *child* voice led to violation of the team contract. My *adult* response prompted the athlete to have a difficult but honest adult conversation with his parents, and ultimately through some assistance from the college's counseling services, work on improving that relationship. The athlete went on to have a happy college career and graduated with no animosity towards me, the team or the program. Because of clear boundaries, accountability, and clear communication, what could have been a negative situation with lasting negative consequences resulted in a positive growth experience for the student.

TYPES OF COMMUNICATION

Over the years of training and practice as a psychologist, much time and effort is dedicated to learning styles and patterns of communication. While on the face of it, effective understanding of communication is quite simple, within the details it is indeed quite complex. One resource I have come to rely on is the excellent book *Interviewing and Change Strategies for Helpers* by Cormier, Nurius, and Oborn (7th edition, 2013), Cengage publishers. What is valuable about this text is that it is based on empirical research. When it comes to our athletes, as with others, there are listening and action responses in our communication.

In listening (which actually includes all senses), non-verbal behavior is important. One need not coach for long before they see a young athlete roll their eyes in response to a coach's request. While eye rolls are easy to note, it is more difficult to note a basketball player whose shoulders are tight upon approach to a free throw. It is common for a young athlete to break form when getting close to a finish line, often as if they are extending their head forward as they look at the finish, and that decreases the runner's efficiency in their use of biomechanics. The athlete is communicating a desire to get to the finish line and not aware of the strategy of maintaining form while in final acceleration.

Indeed, a coach needs peripheral vision to see one athlete's nonverbal behavior when addressing an athlete's colleague. It is indeed easy to say, "Bob, you are going to anchor the 4x4 on Saturday," and not notice Sam's head drop with disappointment (because Sam wanted to anchor and possibly could be a good anchor). If the head drop is noticed, the coach may choose not to address it or may explain to the team the reasons for the current plan. What is most important is the coach noticed the nonverbal communication.

This all becomes more complicated with the addition of gender, as well as racial and cultural differences. An example of cultural difference can be seen in a very young child who came from a culture where boys and girls do not play soccer together. This child, new to the United States, was being out maneuvered by a player and this resulted in significant frustration. During a break the other player removed her baseball cap, revealing she was indeed a girl. This young male athlete ran to the referee, proclaiming in a language the referee did not know that the other team was cheating as they stacked their team with some girls. While this is an obvious example, gender, race and cultural differences can be hard to understand and can result in hurt feelings which will affect performance.

There are three categories of nonverbal behavior: *kinesics* (body motion), *proxemics* and *paralinguistics*. *Kinesics* includes such things as posture, expressions, eye movement (looking at versus looking away) gestures and such. While a coach may not choose to comment on these, it is good to note the athlete who is up front and gesturing to others to 'come over' as coach is talking (an athlete with captain potential down the road). *Proxemics* has to do with personal space. I recall a wonderful young freshman woman who, when timing her laps, would keep at least 10 feet away from the coach and sit at a distance from others. This space diminished as she became more comfortable with the team. Also, she became more expressive and better able to train with other athletes as opposed to her prior preference for solo runs. Again, no comments were made to her, only awareness of her increased comfort and how this enhanced her performance as she became more comfortable with her program and team.

Paralinguistics include such things as verbal quality, intensity, pauses, speech errors and such. For example, you have an athlete who has excellent agility with little endurance and she wants to do the distance hurdles. You tell her that for now she is best suited for 100 meter hurdles and she grits her teeth, tightens her shoulders, looks away and says, "FINE, I WILL RUN THE 100 HURDLES." Unless you can show how combining 100-meter hurdles now and working on distance in the offseason will be an advantage leading to wins in distance hurdles, you likely will have a weakly motivated athlete.

Last, and not mentioned above, is *silence*. Silence motivates the other person to talk and if used judiciously is an excellent communication tool.

The goal of active listening is to utilize all our senses to learn, understand and implement a change. Implementing a change with our athletes is known as "influencing responses." Here, we find six types of responses that influence behavior, each with a different goal and purpose.

Questions (closed). This limits conversation to basic facts such as "How long have you played your sport?" It is intended to acquire information.

Questions (open). Open questions both seek information with elaboration and are facilitative of developing a relationship: "Given your busy schedule this summer, how do you plan to keep up with your summer program?" This provides information to the coach as well as influences the athlete's commitment to do what he/she says can be done.

Information giving. Here we find the coach communicating facts which can be used by the athlete. This is fundamental to athlete learning.

Self- disclosure. This is to be used with care and only for the benefit of the athlete, not as the coach's opportunity to brag about personal accomplishments. It involves sharing personal information with an athlete and it cannot be erased. For example, "Coach, have you ever been injured?" "Yes, and I took a long time to recover because I did not follow the trainer's advice." Here, depending on the athlete, you can see both a possible positive and negative effect of this communication. Another example is, "Coach, I won't be in tomorrow (tears) my grandmother died and the family wants me home." Coach reply (a) "Okay let me know when you are coming back." (b) "I am so sorry, I know how hard it is to lose a loved one. I remember when my grandmother died, it was hard. Let me know when you are back. Please offer the team's sympathies to your family." Clearly the response must fit the coach's and athlete's personality, but the main point is to be aware of how each response can influence the athlete.

Immediacy. This is an example of self-disclosure, of something happening in the moment. "There are two minutes left in the game and I know you are all hurting right now, and you continue to give 100%. I am very proud of you. Two more minutes. Stay consistent and do it together." Pride is the coach's emotion and if the athletes don't like the coach, it can backfire, but usually it is a powerful motivator because it involves emotional sharing in the moment of the game.

Interpretation. This is also referred to as advanced empathic responses. It can be expressed in a number of ways including but not limited to humor, storytelling, paradox and metaphor. Interpretation can make an athlete's implicit message explicit, such as, "I feel you are frustrated to have to work and have little time for practice at home in the summer. Let's make goals that work for you. " As example of a metaphor: "Together we are stronger than any one player, each player is a branch of a solid oak tree." Humor must be used carefully and never aimed in a negative way at one young athlete because it will divide the team and injure the individual. A positive example may be, "Mike, you ran so fast I thought I saw smoke coming out of your racing flats." Note too that while a coach may share a closeness and rapport with a veteran athlete such that the relationship invites ironic humor, other members of the team who are not in on the jokes may take offense on behalf of the athlete or find the humor inappropriate. Paradox can be very useful but can lead to misunderstandings. For example, "The more we are working as a team, the more we see we need to do," or, "If you want to run faster in the 5k you need to slow down (at the start)."

Confrontation. A confrontation is an emotional, sometimes seemingly aggressive interaction. Rather, it is a teasing out of inconsistencies in patterns of two or more behaviors, statements or expressed emotions and presenting them to the person. "Mary, you are a great player. I have noticed in the last three games you seem exhausted in the 4th quarter and your shots are off, yet you say you feel great; please help me understand." Also, "Let's see if we can help you get the energy you need to persevere in the game, I would like you to go to health services for a check-up." Here coach suspects an eating disorder and is wise enough not to diagnose, but rather coach has had conversations with health services/nursing prior to the season where the staff knows if an athlete is sent with a complaint of loss of energy, that when other issues are medically ruled out an eating issue should also be examined by the health care staff, never by the coach even if the coach is a medical professional.

Finally, when questioning your athlete, it is often important to reflect or paraphrase what the athlete said before responding. If the athlete says, "My trainer wants me to give my ankle one more week before I can compete." The coach's response options include (a) "Okay, sit and watch the game and continue to learn the game strategies," or (b) "Your ankle needs more healing time so let's let it heal and you can sit and watch for now. " The second clearly demonstrates to the athlete you are aware, listening and empathic to the need for time to heal. It is important to note athletes often leave the sport when injury separates them from the team. Keeping the athlete included and demonstrating effective listening is a recipe for retention of your athletes.

GOAL SETTING IN SPORTS

Given how complex the art of communication in sports can be, it is no surprise that goal writing can be a challenge. Goal development becomes a relationship contract between coach and athlete and coach and team. While the coach knows what is best for the team, if the team does not buy into the goals, expect no medals at the end of the season.

Yes, we all want to win but winning is the outcome of good goal planning, not the goal itself. To set a goal of winning 80% of your contests is not within your ability to control and it sends a message to your athletes that they are not good enough to take it all. Winning is a desired outcome, not a goal. Goals emphasize what is under your control; winning is a result of setting good goals. There are two types of goals (process and outcome), two groupings (team and athlete), three goal levels (no change, realistic goal, optimal goal), and timing of goals (out of a season and within a season). If properly planned, and accepted by the athlete and team, you have placed your team in an optimal position for a win.

The older and more experienced the team, the more specific the contract becomes with the athlete. I always assumed many of my college players will become coaches, and therefore sought to offer as much detail as possible.

Also, in selecting a goal, it is important for the goal to be sensitive to benefit the athlete. Telling a 13-year-old girl she needs to lose 10 pounds to run faster is not accurate information and is a form of bullying the athlete. Such actions have certainly traumatized many athletes over the years. Athletes often take coach's word as law even if the coach does not think the athlete is listening and this usually has a profound effect on the development of the young person.

Process versus outcome. You may see in preseason that your athletes lack explosive strength as well as agility and decide these improvements will be a goal for early season development (many goals not just one). For explosive strength in jump height you measure the vertical jump in inches and later it will be used to compare to baseline jumps. This difference between the two is your measurement of outcome. For process measures to be used as progress toward outcome you decide to use box jumps and speed hill repeats over x trials and y period of time.

This goal is written along with other goals and communicated with the athletes in such a way as they buy in to the drudgery of hill repetitions. There are many internet examples of goal setting for teams and you can also buy products on the market to facilitate this, but most important is what is available to you given your resources and creative talents.

Another example is the outcome of reducing time in the 100-meter race. The process goals may break down to acceleration out of the blocks in the first 10 meters, speed during the following 60 meters and resisting deceleration in the final 30 meters. For acceleration out of the blocks, process goals may include working on the set position, anticipating the gun and progressions during the first three steps. Process goals feed the outcome goals. Another goal may include managing anxiety, tension or arousal in the blocks prior to the starting gun. The outcome is improving the athlete's 100 meter time. If that time improves and leads to a win, then you reached your desired outcome.

Team and athlete goals. Team goals are a must but it only works if each athlete has agreed to the goals (expectations) based on their talents and motivation at that time. This is time-consuming and detail focused. Team goals need to be measurable and not simply, "Do better than last year." Goals need to be specific and quantifiable such as "improve time to get down court and be in a defense position" or " reduce turn-overs by X%." These are outcome goals and now the team process and individual goals leading to this result need to be established.

Recall, in the first chapter in referencing Hall of Fame coaches, I noted they believe the devil is in the details. Process goals need to be very specific. Achieving these goals puts the team in the best position for a win. For example, the one-week workout plan below (Table 1) was for a specific female athlete with a good background in distance work. The cryptic letters don't matter as they are specific to a sport, but the important point is the devilish details. Again, plans are based on the individual's baseline and this one is an early season race, not the championship segment.

Table 1

	Workout Goal	Mileage	Workout
Monday	VO_2	8	800 - 1200 - 1600 - 1600 - 1200 - 800 (w/ equal rest) @ VO_2 max [5:44 pace] + core

Tuesday	AT	4	@ 65% VO$_2$ max [8:49]
Wednesday	LT	8	6x1000m @ 85% VO2 max w/ 60s rest [6:44] + core
Thursday	AT	5	@ 65% VO$_2$ max [8:49]
Friday	Race (5k)	7	7AM - 20 min — 7PM - 2 up/down - 5k race
Saturday	LR	10	20% week volume (46 miles) @ 65% VO$_2$ max + core
Sunday	AT	4	@ 65% VO$_2$ max [8:49]
			VO$_2$ based on 10k of 38:06

Outcome goals are developed and shared with the athlete and team, but process goals are the coach's information with assignments to the athlete. These process goals are fluid and changing based on circumstances.

Seasons and within a season. Competitive college sports have annual cycles, macro cycles and meso cycles. These become so highly programmed that the NCAA (National Collegiate Athletic Association) provides detailed rules to protect the athlete as to how often (days) and how frequently (within days) an athlete may train with their coach within and out of a season. Here is an example (Graph 1) which is just one aspect of an annual plan that can propel an athlete's skills or burn out the athlete to a sport.

Graph 1

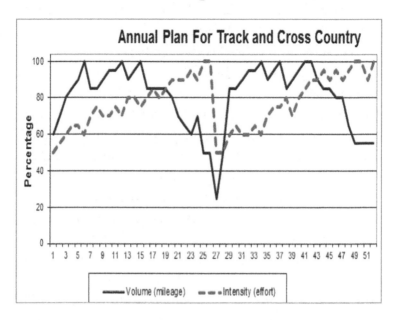

Annual Plan For Track and Cross Country

For the majority of young athletes (90%+) it is important that out of their season they have the opportunity to explore other sports. I know this is heresy to some but the young person needs multiple physical experiences and team and coach experiences. To give a football player instruction for offseason practice and expect him to complete it with joy and exuberance is, for the most part, a fool's journey.

For example, take ten football players at the end of the season and give them a speed training program and take another ten players and have them do spring track with an average coach and guess who will come back faster. Competitors like to compete and therefore giving track meets to athletes will excite and refresh their boring offseason program. This does require sharing information with another coach as well as sharing the athlete, which for some coaches is a challenge to their need to control outcomes. However, the football coach would do well to consider the track coach part of the non-rostered team.

As can be seen from this chapter, to set attainable goals requires not just knowledge of the sport, but awareness that goals need to be focused on process and outcome goals within the season and across seasons for which they are targeted. All this is prefaced on developing ongoing communication and relationships with the athlete to develop goals that are effective and will not fall to poor compliance by the athlete.

Level of Goals. It is recommended that goals have three levels. These levels include: 1) a goal has not been effective and needs to be reevaluated, 2) reasonable growth has occurred and adjustments can be made, 3) the goal has been mastered.

Based on the above, a coach's relationship with their athletes takes time, effort and understanding of the coach/athlete relationship. With that established, the coach is in a position to develop process and outcome goals that include the athlete's baseline skills and motivation. Like developing a financial budget, goals are not written in stone. They are best efforts to plot a course to best advance the individual and team in their growth and development.

Given the complexities of developing a winning team through the establishment and assessment of individual and group goals that are based on knowledge, feelings, motivation and communication, it is recommended that one develops a relationship with a mentor—one who can offer advice specific to your sport and advice on team development and relationships and give feedback about how you are functioning with your team. Also, a mentor can assist when there are challenges of a given athlete's personality, or if the athlete is experiencing difficult emotional issues as discussed in the next chapter.

SEVEN

PERSONALITY AND ABNORMAL PSYCHOLOGY

M any textbooks and thousands of research articles have been produced on the subjects of personality and abnormal behaviors. The focus of this chapter is limited to these two areas as they relate to sports. As a general rule, if certain positive or negative behaviors occur only on the field, then it is for the coach to work with the athlete to engage in a strategy to change the undesirable behavior. If the behaviors occur on and *off* the field (in class, at home, at play) then, while the coach still deals with the behavior as it relates to sports, the coach may have a greater difficulty effecting change with the individual. That said, if you have coached youth for a while, you likely have heard a parent say, "I don't understand why Jason is so organized, well behaved and engaged on the field because that is surely not the behavior we see at home or in school."

Coaches set boundaries for behavior that are very circumscribed and these are both necessary for a winning season and valuable life learning tools for the young athlete. Sometimes, young athletes cannot self-inhibit behaviors that may be distracting or annoying to others, but can inhibit behaviors under the coach's structure and boundaries. As noted in the earlier chapter on the brain, the coach often acts as the prefrontal lobes of the young athlete's brain, areas of the brain responsible for self-control, impulse regulation, organization and planning, to name a few.

The young athlete may demonstrate an increase in such behaviors when they are nervous or anxious, such as is common on a day of competition. That is one reason for game days to be highly structured from when a foot is set on the bus until they are discharged home. Like a pilot entering the airport, nothing is left to chance and behavior is highly organized. On game day, if the athlete is given time to mentally prepare it must be structured as to when it occurs and where.

Further, it is important to note that our young athletes are growing into adults; they are not little adults. It is not okay to label them with a "disordered personality" as their personality is in development. It is best to figure out what works or does not work for them in their role as athlete and then figure how they can contribute to the team. In this capacity you are coach, teacher and mentor directing these young lives.

Last, it is not unusual for a coach to feel, "If only this athlete was not on the team, we would have better team spirit and the team would be easier to coach." This is where a good coach mentor can advise and be of great assistance to you. Sometimes only a five-minute phone call to your mentor can save much distress.

These young athletes need clear direction to perform to the requirements of the coach. Indeed, sometimes our best athletes provide the greatest challenges to the coach relative to integration and team flow. Just ask a college coach if they ever had a high performing athlete whom they would not invite to be a counselor in their summer high school or junior high all sports program. You often will find the answer is a resounding "YES."

PERSONALITY

The definition of personality is partially based on one's overall theory of personality—and there are many theories. When one describes a person's personality, they are usually describing a stable, consistent behavior known as a trait. Generally they are not describing a specific state, which a person may be exhibiting at any given time.

It has been thought that if we could predict a person's capacity to win in any given sport based on their personality, then we could administer a personality test and select athletes based on their ability to win. While this would make life easy, I am not aware of research conclusively documenting the ability to predict a win based on personality.

Though there are certain characteristics commonly found among elite athletes, the longitudinal predictive studies are not available that predict success. Literature about elite athletes points to increased mental toughness, perfectionism, resilience and motivation among other traits. However, those who work with elite athletes know that group data do not always apply to their talented athlete. One study states the elite athlete has low anxiety and yet an Olympic psychologist relayed the story of a young teen who in the Olympic village became highly anxious because she could not find her toothbrush. While there may be more consistency of personality among elite athletes, the variance is still strong. Further, when studying the personality of elite athletes it is not known whether personality is molded by the behavior necessary to become an elite athlete, or the personality facilitates the process to become elite, or a combination of both.

What stands out in recent research is "The Big Five" factor theory of personality. These five factors include: openness to experience, conscientiousness, extraversion, agreeableness and neuroticism. A few studies found the successful student athlete scores higher on agreeableness, conscientiousness and emotional stability. Also, burnout was associated with perfectionism. While this and related research is very intriguing, it does not necessarily predict future performance of a young athlete; rather, it is correlated with success. It does inform the coach that a well-structured and carefully planned program with informed athletes who are 'on board' with the program may put the team in a better position to win (see chapter on goal setting). But it also tells us that reinforcing perfectionism over the enjoyment of the sport could lead to either problems and reduced love of the sport.

Some research shows the athlete's personality characteristics may be useful in predicting the coach-athlete relationship. However, on the college level, athletes are recruited and this is a screening mechanism that can bias any research. Assuming financial aid is sufficient and it is the type of college the student is interested in attending, some athletes on college interview like a supportive coach and others may like one who appears gruff. This self-selection can influence any subsequent data collection.

While research developments in sport psychology are very interesting, much research is relatively new and ongoing. For example, areas under study include: genetics, personality, injury recovery, burnout, hardiness and goal compliance. We are a long way from being able to predict with any certitude who will succeed in a specific sport based on personality traits.

Beyond the trait approach, there are other orientations to personality theory. Humanistic Psychology offers a value-based approach to valuation of the person. The Psychology of Learning and Motivation offers very specific details for managing athlete behavior. And there is a growing appreciation for the athlete's phenomenology, or how the athlete structures their awareness of the world and its meaning in how they view the world. The bottom line for now is that for our young, developing athletes, labeling them with a negative personality trait or other designation will more likely produce a self-fulfilling prophecy (they will become who the coach thinks they are), and they are too young to be given a label that will follow them in life.

ABNORMAL PSYCHOLOGY

There are many textbooks titled "Abnormal Psychology" and they are well organized by topic area including definition, assessment and standard interventions. However, prior to discussing abnormal psychology, it is of value to present a brief view of normal behavior, as without an appreciation of "normal" it is not possible to get a sense of when an athlete is having difficulty in their life.

Normal behavior is often described as a statistical mean. While this may be empirically accurate, it would suggest that a person who is not part of the dominant culture is statistically not normal and their behavior should be addressed. This can have negative and unwanted implications for the athlete and the team. For example, there is a time when one's cultural variants need to be respected and explored to advantage the athlete in her or his sport. Also, variations in mood are a normal part of life to which most people learn to form adjustments and continue to function in their environment. It is when variation from the norm disables a person that their behavior may be categorized as "abnormal." Regarding normal behavior, in general, "normal" is viewed as:

The ability to form meaningful social relationships. Someone living an isolated life by choice and who is comfortable with the choice is not abnormal. It is when a person cannot develop and sustain meaningful social relationships that their behavior is not adaptive for them and as a result has negative consequences.

The ability to adapt to frustration or loss. When a loved one dies there is a usual period of grief and sadness when the person may lose sleep, feel depressed and have a decreased or increased appetite. The normal person recovers within a reasonable period of time and though they may still grieve, they gradually return to normal behaviors, sleep and diet. Similarly, a person who missed the tie breaking free throw or a person who got cut from a team should be able to bounce back in a reasonable period of time.

The ability to maintain a daily routine of work or school and social/leisure activities. For example, a student athlete had good grades in the fall. After feeling they let the team down by missing the shot on goal during the championship game, they are failing classes in the spring. Also, there are increased absences from school. This athlete is a prime candidate to refer for mental health assistance.

Depression is to mental health care as the common cold is to medical care. Most often good self-care or support from friends or family is sufficient to rebound and get on with life. It is when the person cannot make adjustments within a reasonable period of time that help is to be offered.

Also, it is best not to say, "You're depressed," or such other negative descriptors. What is often best is to describe the behavior, such as, "Steve, since your father died you have had trouble with school, your attendance is off and you are isolating yourself from your friends. It has been three months now and it may be time for us to think about what we can do to help you get on track again…" This latter example does not make the person feel they "have" depression, which can often engender embarrassment or even shame; rather, it describes what he "does" that can be addressed with assistance. "Has" versus "does" may not seem important but one labels the person ("he is a lazy person") and the other labels the behavior ("he moves slowly in practice and is the last to show up.")

The treatment is the same but the sense of self may be different. Consider "I am dumb" versus "I did poorly on this exam," or "I am a depressed person" versus "My behavior since my father died has not been working for me. I don't want to cry every day and I don't want to isolate."

Mental health issues on a team are best treated in the same manner as metabolic or neuromuscular issues. That is, maintain team organization, structure and boundaries and accommodate any disability based on the direction of the health care or mental health provider's prescribed accommodations. This is where good relationships with the non-rostered team members are important.

For example, you would respect and support the needs of the diabetic child to manage their diabetes according to their prescribed care. The same is also true for the young athlete with a mental health issue. When a young athlete is on medication for a mental health issue there are periods of adjustment and usually a period of re-adjustment. Even when the youth is stable on medications, changes in extended physical exertion or periods of significant stress, emotional or environmental (such as progressive dehydration on long summer days) may affect adjustment to certain medications and the youth may have "bad days."

When someone is struggling with mental health issues it is often a comfort for the person to have a time of day when activities are predictable and structured and they are working in an environment of people they believe care about them. Indeed, as noted earlier, on the college level students often do better academically when they are in season than out of season. Many attribute this to the structure required of being at practice at 4:00 each day and the necessity of organizing their day to accommodate practice. In addition, time spent with fellow teammates before practice starts and after it ends is often highly valued by the athletes.

A specific example of issues in health care of the athlete is eating disorders. In considering this area, recall the above; if the behavior only occurs on the field and in no other area of the young athlete's life, then it is important to look at team culture and coach generated disorders. Writing "coach generated disorder" is indeed a bit unfair as coaches don't intend to cause distress and certainly there are athletes who are vulnerable and don't require much to become disordered in their eating, but this is critically important to be aware of in the development of the young athlete.

Here are two situations with very different outcomes. Coach Jade is beginning a cross country season and knows the ages of her athletes (11-14). The athletes are sufficiently young that she will be limiting mileage and the hard workouts will be, as much as possible, based on fun activities. As the season starts she invites athletes and family to a meeting where they are handed a list of healthy foods one may choose to eat before a meet and a general list of recovery foods. Ideally, she tried to have a registered dietician come to speak but that did not work out at this time. She tells the young team that each person is unique and she will work with the team to develop his or her best inner talents and skills. She will answer their questions but does not judge. Indeed, there is something about endurance athletes and Pop-Tarts that appear inseparable. Her team learns that chocolate milk is terrible before a hard workout but wonderful after the workout. Her team has a great season.

In the second situation, Coach Mike attended a large regional conference where a winning coach spoke to a crowd about maintaining a food diary for the athletes. Coach Mike wants his team to do well and places them on a running schedule that is above their years of development with a result of mid-season injuries. He has the athletes maintain food diaries which he dutifully reviews each week. He does not notice the athletes are entering logs with the same pen and same pressure, indicating likely they completed the journal all at once before coming to turn in their weekly food log.

Janice, however, is very dutiful in completing her journal as she is not sure she is a good athlete but wants to be tops on the team. The coach looks at her diary and says, "Janice, you had a weak workout today because the Pop-Tarts are empty calories." For many people, saying "empty calories" and "you are fat" are the same thing. This is not at all what Coach Mike intended. In addition, Janice has a slow workout because she felt fat and does not look like Suzy, who is slim and gets a lot of Coach Mike's attention because she is really fast. Janice internalizes the message: I am ugly.

Coach Mike goes home believing he is helping Janice and Janice goes home with increased self-assurance that she needs to lose weight if she wants to be good as an athlete and feel good about herself. As she rapidly loses weight she metabolically slows and her performance does not improve, so she continues her journey until, eventually at 17 her physician diagnoses the "female triad," where she has decreased energy, menstrual difficulties and low bone density. There are gender differences in how athletes respond to coaches and this is discussed in the chapter on gender. In addition, team culture may reinforce negative self-beliefs and if this culture is not addressed, it can be very toxic.

Granted, I have simplified this example. Yet a coach's contribution to an athlete's disorder, inadvertent though it may be, can be like a snowball rolling down the hill. As a coach, I have had a number of quality high school athletes who decide not to compete in college because "I want the whole college experience and playing a sport won't give that to me." On casual follow up as college juniors or seniors (remember, I also teach and likely will see them again) they admit to having burned out in high school on the sport they initially loved.

As a follow up to this example consider the football player told by the coach, "You need to bulk up; you need to eat 3500 calories a day in carbs and protein or you are just going to be pushed around on the field. Don't be a wimp, bulk up." For these young athletes the effects on the physical health of the person may be more delayed, but obesity has lifelong devastating effects. It is a very different message to say, "Let's set a plan to work on ballistic strength and line strategy and in consultation let's get our trainers and nutritionist to help with balancing ballistic workouts with nutrition that will assist in building strength on the line." While this may lead to a conversation about the negative value of endogenous steroids to facilitate growth, there needs to be clear team culture surrounding education and acceptance of the healthy path to physical neuromuscular development.

In addition to the examples above is the young athlete who comes to the team with an eating disorder of either certain or unknown origin. I have seen a mother at a summer camp making body-shaming comments about her daughter in front of the coach. The mother also had a self-reported eating disorder and said, "I am trying to help her be the best person she can be." I have also seen eating issues emerge from an athlete's self-attempt to lose weight due to feeling anxious and depressed and once the weight is lost people tell the person they are too skinny, given the person went from 120 down to 90 pounds. When the person puts on five pounds they do perceptually feel fat but their world tells them they are just confused and need to gain more weight. So, what began as a journey with anxiety and/or depression becomes, in addition, a social dilemma of "I feel fat and they want me to gain more weight and as a result I feel increased shame and embarrassment." Granted, eating disorders are more complex, but this example represents experiences that are far too common.

As you can see, whether an eating issue has its origins on the team or is presented to the team as a pre-existing condition, an eating disorder is a serious health condition that is beyond the training of the coach. In my career I have worked professionally with eating disordered individuals and it is indeed both complex and generally requires a multidimensional team approach. I always have kept the distinction clear between my work as coach and as a psychologist. On the occasion when a student athlete presents to college with a disorder I assure and reassure them I will be their coach and I need for them to work with college health and counseling services as well as the team training staff to direct their health care. My communication with these services is as a coach receiving their direction to best assist the athlete.

For the athlete with an eating disorder, generally there is co-existing depression, anxiety and often conflict with others as well as self-shaming behaviors. For these reasons, I do not address eating issues any more than I would address diabetes management with the athletes. I do not have them keep journals. Body shaming is all too common today. For example, Coach Salazar, a top tier athlete and coach to elite athletes, is reported to have coached track prodigy Mary Cain to a life-threatening eating disorder.

While the athlete's weight is assessed at health services, there should never be a team "weigh in" as weight is a personal measurement, as are blood sugar and intracellular iron levels. Nutrition is discussed in general at the start of the season and specific questions are answered as they arise and with great care.

At a national conference, a number of coaches admitted to giving zinc lollipops to their team. This can be considered practicing medicine without a license. Referral to a professional experienced with athletes can be difficult to come by but is of significant value to the team and the athletes.

For example, when an athlete is complaining of inability to recover normally and is running more than one or two days with elevated morning heart rates and complains of heaviness in the legs, it is typical for them to have an iron test. Many will say iron is normal but with a health care person experienced with endurance athletes, a ferritin test can indicate low intracellular iron, which can be corrected. What is most important is that you assist your athletes in finding professionals trained to work with endurance athletes and then let them do their job.

The coach therefore cares for anxiety, depression, eating issues, body dysmorphic disorders and such by providing a structured environment with clear boundaries and expectations within a nurturing environment with clearly defined consequences established in preseason. For example, a team member just lost a parent. The team members and coach sent cards and some attended the service. As the athlete returned to the team the coach said, "We are glad to see you and welcome back. Are you ready to work? Okay, let us know if you need anything." Then the person is treated just as any other team member with the coach perhaps allowing some leeway on first day back, but by game day the athlete gets entered based on readiness to compete.

Regarding substance use or abuse, the boundaries are clearly set. No performance enhancing drugs. No non-prescribed medications. Law does not allow use of alcohol for those under age 21. Athletes have team meetings with captains to agree on those areas that are not covered by law or rule. If athletes are using banned substances they will be removed from competition until cleared by medical staff and they will attend a program to address substance misuse or addiction. A second occasion is a statement to the coach and team that they chose substance misuse over team and their decision to leave the team would be respected. On the rare occasion when this has happened, I informed the athlete that I cared about them as a person (and I do), and the substance issue was so critical to their wellbeing that I held them above the team and hoped they would get the assistance they needed.

In summary, our young athletes need boundaries, nurturing, discipline and consistency. During practice, all thoughts focus on the workout and this does give a temporary reprieve to someone who is anxious or depressed. In the end, it is good therapy for them; it is time out from their distress and the activity component provides for better sleep, and improved sleep helps with managing anxiety, depression and other issues.

Young athletes seek to be liked by their coach and at the same time are concerned with feeling rejected or inadequate. Any comment about their mood, body size and personal dietary habits can have long-ranging and negative consequences. Also, preseason is the time to have professional guests to talk and disseminate pamphlets, as well as for the coach to hand out general pamphlets to all athletes (such as pre-competition, general sport-specific food suggestions and recovery suggestions).

Remember also, science generally addresses the norm, not the individual. What is recommended as best practice is not always best for a specific individual. I once had an athlete who ran marathons. Her best one was the day following an evening indiscretion of a large banana split with chocolate sauce. She ran with joy and so happened to have her PR in that marathon and qualified for Boston. She did run many other marathons but this was her best. Keeping the sport ENJOYABLE is of great value to the athlete and enhances the likelihood of a win.

A few final notes. It is not uncommon for the athlete with personal difficulties to self-isolate or to engage in acting out behaviors that can be disruptive. It is important to keep the athlete engaged on and off the field. By off the field, it is meant in the bus, during breaks or immediately prior to or following practice. Next, it is not uncommon for schools to give the coach an envelope with the health statuses of his or her athletes to be used during an away game should there be an injury. These may also contain mental health diagnoses that are important should the athlete require treatment for an injury and is on psychotropic medications. These envelopes should remain sealed and not opened by the coach unless necessity demands it be opened, It is incredibly hard to not be aware of a trauma history, bipolar depression and such when an athlete's behavior is not in line with the team. Once an athlete's mental health history is seen, it cannot be unseen by a coach. Your job is to see each athlete as the person who shows up to practice and games, to hold each athlete to the standards set at preseason, and to do so in a balanced, nurturing manner of accepting the person but holding him or her accountable for their behavior.

Last, it is not unusual to view a personality issue or "abnormal" when in fact it is cultural or gender specific. This mistake in optics can be damaging to the person and the team.

EIGHT

GENDER AND CULTURE

GENDER

Historically, the coaching of sports was a male dominated industry. Today, we are seeing increasing numbers of women coaching at all levels and types of sport. Throughout my years as a coach, I have found it fascinating to watch reactions of men in athletics respond to women coaches. There are thousands of stories of good male coaches who have had a wonderful impact on many athletes' lives. It is the few negative coaches who stand out as poor examples. In the early days you would hear comments related to suggestions as to a female coach's sexual preference. (Any male of a certain age has witnessed more than one juvenile wink-and-nod lesbian joke.) That seems now like a long time ago, but it wasn't. It was a time of growth through ignorance and prejudice not far removed from the ignorant idea that women could not run a marathon without compromising their reproductive capacity.

While we have made progress in gender equity in coaching we are far from attaining a healthy gender balance. For example, I know two nationally ranked coaches of similar age and talent. I have respect for both coaches. I have heard the male coach described as tough, disciplined, demanding and overall a solid coach. I have heard the female coach described in a similar fashion, but in addition I have also heard the term "bitch" applied to her. The authoritative male continues to be seen differently than the authoritative female, especially if they are both winning coaches.

Granted it is not at all unusual when a coach's team is beaten by another coach to quietly feel the winning coach must be cheating, or is favored with superior athletes, or has a better budget. Sometimes, for a male coach to be beaten by a female coach, it can be very provocative and bring forward many negative feelings in the male coach. Hopefully, time, exposure and self-inhibition of rude comments, coupled with continued development of mutual respect, will facilitate continued positive change.

Recall from earlier chapters, the athlete takes the win, not the coach. If the athlete does everything he or she is asked to do by the coach and the team loses, the loss goes to the coach. Recall also, the Hall of Fame coach continues to strive to learn and, in this regard, befriending a winning coach (male or female) is something to consider. Men have had opportunities for leadership in the field for much longer, but in time more and more female mentors will be available in every sport.

Regarding athletes, I have seen many male coaches attempt to coach female athletes in the same manner they coach male athletes. This usually leads to frustration and confusion on the part of the coach. I offer the following example of a Hall of Fame coach who was quite advanced in age, and is a highly successful Division I coach. His coaching occurred prior to the 1950s. He spoke with great and fond memories of his male athletes, as well as discussion of equipment and challenges of the early days of coaching athletes. When asked if he had coached any females, he leaned back and said, "Oh my gosh, no. Girls cry."

At that time assumptions about gender roles were pre-defined and it was safely assumed girls were made of "sugar and spice and everything nice" and boys were made of "snips and snails and puppy dog tails." Indeed, the textbooks were speaking of biologists and chemists as he or him and homemakers or florists as she or her. Those were difficult times indeed for a young girl to dream of being a basketball player or a wrestler.

Change does occur over time, though it appears a slow process to achieve change. I recall watching a young mother of a junior high female athlete who saw her daughter drop to the ground on her knees about 150 meters from the finish line, whereupon the mother yelled, "Get up and finish this race!" She yelled multiple times to her daughter and the daughter slowly rose and staggered to the finish line, where her mother greeted her with hugs, water and a towel. The daughter appeared proud of her completion of the event and was embracing her mother. Not too many years ago observers would have frowned on this mother's behavior.

Based on my experiences over the years, many male coaches who started their career coaching males found the transition to coaching females as a difficult learning curve because what applies to young men does not always apply to young women. This is not to say that gender roles are fixed and unchanging over time. Rather, there appear to be some differences that need to be attended to while the coaching industry continues to grow and develop.

Regarding differences between genders, it is difficult to predict for any given team as there are very wide variations within each gender. For example, in one summer camp I had two 5th graders come to the camp for the first time. Both campers were male. The first was dropped off and as his mother started driving away he said to her, "What kind of camp is this?" While slowly accelerating she answered, "It's a running camp." He began to run, all right, chasing the car while screaming, "I don't want to run!" He was hefty in size and admitted he never ran, which was inconsistent with the application form mother had completed. I assured him he did not have to run and he could sit by the tree and watch others work out and learn by watching.

On this warm day, we paired up the 5th graders with each other and told them they were doing a circuit run with water balloons, passing them back and forth as they ran the circuit. This young man got up from the shade of the tree and exclaimed, "I want to play too!" He joined in and each child played within their tolerances with additional structured runs in the afternoon for advanced runners, while others watched a movie about running.

The second child, also a 5th grader, came ready to run. He could discuss running shoes and why he wore this type of shoe and for what purpose. He read about great runners who were his idols. In the afternoon runs he kept up with the high school freshmen. Our counselor, a college athlete who was running with the group, had to hold him back as he was quite competitive and we did not want to send injured athletes back to their coaches for the start of preseason.

When his mother came to pick him up he ran to the car saying in a loud voice, "Mom, I love this camp, THERE ARE OTHER PEOPLE LIKE ME!" They lived in a rural area and he was the only runner in his neighborhood. He returned to camp the next year and eventually went on to a DI college program.

Clearly, each child is unique and therefore gender comparisons have many disadvantages due to the large differences within each gender. And yet, comparisons appear to exist to the capacity that many good male coaches cannot, or chose not to make a transition from coaching boys or men to coaching girls or women.

One example I had not seen with boys comes from another summer camp experience. There was a 5th grade girl who took off on a trail run with her group. Shortly thereafter, her college student counselor called in saying they were in the back field and this young athlete had rolled her ankle and was not able to run back. I took a female counselor with me in my jeep and we drove cross-country across the trails to the field where she was injured. The counselor helped her into the back of the jeep whereupon we drove to the trainer's office. I should note it was a warm sunny day and the top of the jeep was down. As we drove to the gym where the trainers worked, the other campers had returned and saw her in the jeep with coach and the female college athlete.

The next day the camper returned with a wrapped ankle and crutches. Once we started practice, another young female camper said, "I don't feel good, can I go sit?" I said yes to her and within five minutes a second camper had the same complaint. Given it is unusual to have two ill campers with the same complaint, I watched her go sit and to my surprise both were sitting in my jeep waiting for a wonderful, top down jeep transfer with the coach and the female college athlete. Acting as if I did not notice, a third child, another female camper, took ill, per her verbal self-report, and scurried off to the jeep. I asked a college counselor to give them water and then announced in a loud voice we were going to do an exercise most distance runners love. To my surprise all three recovered and joined the group.

As it turned out, all three knew each other and admitted to a female college counselor that they wanted a ride in the jeep and the attention of the coach. While it is not impossible to imagine young male junior high athletes doing this, it is indeed far less probable.

We know from literature and experience that women tend to be more relationship and process focused and men tend to be more outcome focused, though hopefully this is continuing to change over time. In discussion with a high school coach who has won numerous titles and coaches both male and female athletes, she shared the following observations. Regardless of gender, it is important to always tell the truth to the athletes. The difference is generally the male athlete can be directly challenged and the female needs to evaluate the process. For example, for the male: "Coach, why was my 800 meter time off by 2 seconds?" Coach reply: "You tell me what happened out there and we will talk about it." For the female: "Coach, why was my 800 meter time off by 2 seconds?" Coach: "After the first lap your running form broke down and that cost you time, we will work with that in training."

Also, it can be easier to train men as a platoon. The group gets the task and carries it out as a group. If the coach singles out an athlete for discipline, the athlete may say to others later, "Do you believe what coach did to me?" to which others are more likely to respond, "Yeah, that stinks," and they then get on with whatever they are doing. They are not likely to process the experience further in terms of,

"What do you think the coach meant?" or "I don't think the coach likes you," or related questions and comments.

As a group, the female athletes are often likely to process the relationship component and have subgroups they can go to for discussion. In this situation, when a coach disciplines an athlete, the athlete may turn to her subgroup later for emotional support and she is likely to get much more of a response from them than, "Yeah, that stinks." This processing of relationships and events can readily lead to divisions and subgroups.

When a coach hears, "Mary and Jane are upset with the Captain, " it is easy for the coach to think, "I don't like coaching girls, there is too much drama." This is a convenient rationalization, not an explanation. An experienced coach will set the stage during preseason for dealing with subgroup differences and in season have a means for addressing issues as they occur and not simply use the pejorative term "drama." Having an assistant coach can be very helpful in managing relationships and assisting with team cohesion.

Another difference is that the young female athlete is more responsive to the term "trust the process," whereas often the male athlete wants to know the coach's credentials and success with other athletes. The young woman typically needs to ask questions about what the purpose of such and such is and how it relates to the desired outcome. She seeks a coach/athlete relationship with knowledge of a process she can understand. The male athlete more often wants to know the coach has the right stuff and then he can trust the program. The former is logical and relational and the latter is qualification centered and outcome focused.

Clearly, as noted above, variations within gender are sufficiently broad such that it can, be difficult at times to note variations between genders. However, male coaches who don't make the transition from male to female athletes will often describe females as emotional and drama driven, which fundamentally means it may be a good time to talk with one who has successfully coached female athletes—a mentor.

I have seen quality coaches who can adapt to coaching male or female athletes and I have asked whether male coaches find it more difficult coaching female athletes, or female coaches coaching male athletes. This question often results in silence and conjecture. What does appear clear to me is that men have been coaching longer than women and mostly coaching male athletes. As a result they may be more likely to try to apply what they have learned from their male teams to female athletes. This can be a recipe for a difficult transition. My advice from other chapters applies here. When first coaching a sport or a different gender than you have coached before, get a mentor. (I know I have said this before but it merits repetition.) Also, get an assistant (preferably one with different experiences than you) who can provide feedback and be a witness to your good work as well as help guide you from missteps.

On a separate topic, having coached female athletes on distance events, I often noticed them discussing weight, food and calories. The idea that a distance runner had to be light of weight had been an accepted assumption over time and reinforced by many coaches all the way up to coaching the elite athlete. Young women coming to college with hidden weight concerns often appeared to have little or no work with strength training. Proper strength training that does not compromise flexibility adds to running efficiency, and when matched with running economy places the athlete in the best position for a personal record. Sadly, as I noted in the previous chapter, self-shaming and body shaming by the coach, however unintended, continues in athletics and reinforces weight concerns.

One example of a successful transition to healthy eating and healthy body image was a young woman who came to college believing thin is better for a distance runner. While she and others did not have an eating disorder, they did learn the myth that light is right for women. With strength training, her already normal self-esteem further developed, as did her race time. On one spring afternoon while heading out to train, I noticed the sleeves of her shirt rolled up and she was flexing her biceps and smiling saying to her teammates, "Sun's out, guns out." Competent age-specific strength training by a nationally certified strength and conditioning coach is empowering for both male and female athletes. It also sets a healthy standard for self-respect, personal growth and a lifetime of health.

While we are aware of the negative effects of weight comments to a young female athlete, we appear unaware of the effects of similar comments to male athletes. To say to a male athlete "You are too skinny, you need to put on 30 pounds" is body shaming, as I noted earlier.

Another area where good mentorship can be very valuable is in working with athletes who self-describes as any of LGBTQIAP. If you act in the best interest and concern for your athlete as a person, you will have taken an incredibly important step in helping your athlete.

When you set your expectations in preseason stick with them. Still, it is difficult when a captain comes to you saying, "Coach, Mary told her parents she is gay and they kicked her out of the house and she is depressed and that is why she is having trouble at practice." Having worked as a professional with young people in this type of situation I will say, the psychologist and the coach are different professions and one should not cloud the other. Treat the person with respect and dignity. Hold them to their practice and perhaps they will have one place in their life during this difficult time where they know they can practice, exercise and have their friends; a place where they do not have to deal with (or minimally have to deal with) the stress, anxiety or depression of being rejected for who they are as a person.

Encouraging a referral of a person who is suffering parental rejection to the proper resource for assistance during this important time in their life, is as important as getting assistance from a health care provider on how to work with a diabetic on the team. I would not address her suffering with the athlete; rather, I would inform the athlete that I had noticed changes in her performance and ask if I can help. Or, in this case where the captain mentioned the concern, ask the athlete if there are things going on off the practice field that affect practice. If she says yes, that opens the door to gentle referral to a school counselor or other professional for assistance. Again, keep the practice a safe place for this young athlete, and all the athletes, to exercise, learn and have their friends. Let her have a memory of you as someone who cared for her as a person. I have known clients in my practice for whom the coach's respect was a stabilizer, and sometimes the only stabilizer, in their ship transitioning through the stormy waters of adolescence.

Also, I would advise that in preseason you set ground rules that you and your assistant don't keep secrets, and that when something occurs that is not coaching related you will each direct the person to the proper place. It sets a clear and necessary boundary. If they ask for assistance or if the captain asks, you can point them in the proper direction for help. Then, return to practice. Any procedures for documentation, if required and necessary, should be established ahead of time. Turn it over to the professional and don't get in the middle of a hornet's nest of a family concern, but do give respect and dignity to the struggling youth and be their coach. Indeed, it may get you in trouble with the family just to refer to a school counselor. Seek advice from your mentor.

It is very important to be aware of your own biases, stereotypes and self-judgments and it is best you don't let these have a negative influence on the young athlete. It is a good idea to discuss sensitive conversations with your authorities so that in the event a parent should call the school asking why the coach is not siding with them your authorities will be able to explain your coaching position. Or course, this assumes you took the time to develop your relationship with your authorities prior to the season.

Moving to more scientific based research on gender, the Women's Sports Foundation[5] reports on a national survey they commissioned which investigated participation and experiences of girls in youth sports. This was done relative to coaching. The study was based on experts in the area and received results from each of 1129 girls (ages 7-13) and their parents. The study, titled, "Coaching Through a Gender Lens: Maximizing Girls' Play and Potential," is found on their web page. It is an excellent resource with good information for coaches.

When these young athletes were asked what they liked about playing sports, winning was tied for 7th place with having a good coach. The top two reasons for playing a sport

5. https://www.womenssportsfoundation.org

are making friends and being part of a team. Should a coach focus on the win to the exclusion of the social/interpersonal aspects of being on a team, the probability of a 'win' likely is reduced, as the athletes may not be motivated as a team to strongly pursue the win.

This study also reported that girls are more likely than boys to be self-critical, more conscious of their body and more likely to compare themselves to others. Indeed, this can affect whether a young girl continues in sports or drops out. Also, many of the young athletes reported worrying about being better than their teammates. The wise coach is aware of the possibility of a concern about being excluded from the group as being different, a better athlete in this instance.

As an aside, it is of value to note male coaches who are not aware of, and as a result do not focus on team culture and athlete self-identity, may have considerable difficulty feeling effective as a coach. Such a lapse can easily lead us back to the comments above about "too much drama."

The study recommends a developmental, mastery-based approach to coaching as well as "the importance of coaches being positive and promoting (emphasizing, valuing) goals of fun, effort, dedication, and skill development. Effective coaches view mistakes as opportunities to learn and adjust, and provide good technical instruction" (P.34). Note, this is a consistent theme found throughout this text and I believe it applies equally to boys, though the study was limited to girls.

CULTURE

Building a positive team culture is foundational to building a winning season. When building a team, the culture is often developed with teammates from different cultural and racial backgrounds. A team develops its own language (tennis= love, baseball = grand slam, football= 3rd down and 8, hockey = blue line and so on); its own sub-culture of literature, film, and oral history; its own chants and songs, and its own uniforms. Most important, team culture involves values and beliefs relative to how one behaves as an individual and as a group in matters of victory and defeat. As such, the team has prescribed ethics (by the commission or school) and personal ethics formulated and /or supported by the coach.

Indeed a well-formed team culture brings people together. As basketball great Kareem Abdul-Jabbar has noted with great insight: "Sports is one of the few areas in which Americans of all races can talk to each other. Right now, it may be the country's best hope for meaningful dialogue."

The team culture can bring discordant cultures and races together in one group and, as a result, rise above differences and develop a sense of community. I believe this culture formation is considerably more powerful than an attempt to change attitudes or beliefs with a lecture or series of lectures on culture. However, the combination of both can be a formidable tool to improve relationships among people.

Nelson Mandela, former president in South Africa, saw sports as a weapon against racism and thought sports had the ability to change the world: "[Sport] has the power to inspire. It has the power to unite people in a way that little else does. It speaks to youth in a language they understand." Mandela attained the privilege of his country to host the World Cup finals in 2010. This success was seen as a victory in helping to unite a racially divided country.

While reading this, you may think it is wonderful that Mandela could unite his country through sport, but you are simply coaching a baseball team of 12 children. How is that important? And yet, you know the answer. These children are our future and you have a powerful ability to make a difference in how you respond as a role model for positive change. Even if your team lacks obvious diversity, there will be diversity in your competition and in the bleachers as well as diversity issues that are not immediately obvious to you.

The fact that you develop, mold and control team culture is both foundational to the big win and a life mentoring opportunity for our developing adolescent athletes. Though what we say is important and can have lasting effects on our athletes, mentoring is done more through example and formative team experiences than through words.

As a coach you can certainly pride yourself in believing you are not prejudiced and don't tolerate prejudice on your team. However, it is the bias or prejudice we don't know that can be hurtful in a manner not intended as a coach. This is especially true if you are part of the "privileged" white class.

As a self-disclosure, when I was young, I would have said I am not privileged. I came from a large loving family and was raised on food stamps. I was part of the first generation in my family to attend college and worked three jobs while studying in college. One day, some years ago, someone said to me, you are where you are because you are privileged. The tone of their voice, combined with my sense of hard work to attain a challenging goal, rendered me frustrated with hurt feelings. A couple weeks later I asked a friend about "white male privilege" and was impressed with my ignorance. Indeed, privilege does not recognize privilege. This in no way diminishes my hard work or my family's many sacrifices, but it has become clear to me that while I worked hard for my accomplishments, I had clear advantages.

While many families lack resources for college, some are able to secure loans tied to their property as a guarantee. If the grandparents of a minority student interested in college were "red lined" and banks therefore left them out of home purchasing in desirable neighborhoods, the financial implications continue across generations and have the capacity to limit access to funding for education. Even today, many are encouraged to do "online" learning, as it is cheaper. Those who can afford it will have an education on campus with mentors physically present who can know the student and write recommendations for jobs and graduate study, as well as help guide them in their academic development in a manner not readily available to many online students. While the online option is good for many people, it cannot become the sole resource for the marginalized.

Regarding gender privilege, there is older research indicating male college students receive more eye contact and attention by their faculty than females in the class, a clear advantage. The male athlete with a male coach is privileged to have a coach who understands him while a female athlete with a male coach whose history was working with male athletes, may struggle with her coach's understanding of her as an individual.

Some years ago, a study revealed that senior athletic training staff would generally get the male athletes while female athletes received the newer trainers. While not a planned conspiracy, senior staff worked with male athletes before Title 9 took effect and brought more teams to the fields and often it appeared a continuation of comfort with the sport and gender they worked with over time. Also, in

2020, a young female trainer who has a solid reputation and works in an excellent high school program said what while applying for work, two potential employers told her they would not hire a woman.

One last example is one of a subtle geographic bias affecting judgment of an athlete. I spent a few years in the southern United States and noted when sprinters completed a hard sprint and needed about three minutes recovery time from an anaerobic exercise, they would often go into the shade to recover. Later, living in the north where we had a few football recruits from the south, when they completed an anaerobic trial they walked into the shade and stood there. Generally our athletes would walk, not stand around in the shade. A new assistant commented, "They appear lazy." I asked the assistant to ask them why they were just standing there and they did not have a good answer. I asked them what they did in high school in Alabama on a hot sunny day and they said they would get out of the sun. It was such a habit they did not recognize their behavior any more than children from New Hampshire would notice themselves stomping when they walk in a door to knock the snow off their boots.

These young men were not being lazy. They were practicing a behavior conditioned in high school, and probably long before that, that transferred into their new environment. If there was no attempt to understand, they could have been labeled as lazy and receive all the responses a coach may give to athletes perceived as lazy. This reinforces our need to get to know our athletes and their world through communication with them and through expanding our own world meaning and experiences.

Basically, this relates back to the idea that as coaches we assume the incredible responsibility of careful development of a winning team culture that brings forward our best mentoring and which positions the athletes into a winning scenario as well as a life learning opportunity. To understand our athlete, it is best to seek to understand our own history and continue to learn from others. What a privilege it is to coach our young. What a challenge to learn all the fundamentals of coaching a sport and develop youth of all backgrounds and identities into young adults who will reach across barriers to shape better communities for our future. Sports may be, as Kareem so eloquently said, "the country's best hope."

NINE

MOTIVATION, PERFORMANCE, AND SPORT INTERVENTIONS

The study of motivation can appear quite simple and yet like the other aspects of human behavior discussed in this book, it is incredibly complex. To speak of motivation within sports we need to look at it as a multidimensional concept. In the chapter that follows I focus upon athletic readiness, making a clear distinction between the two kinds: neuromuscular readiness and central nervous system readiness.

For our purposes we will refer to these as physiological readiness and cognitive readiness, even though of course thinking is a physical activity. As we consider the kinds of preparation needed for optimal athletic performance and the best techniques for achieving this, I am mindful that, while some things are constant, there can be great differences, depending on the type of sport played. Managing motivation, being "psyched up" and mentally on point, is quite different in hockey than in golf or the winter biathlon (physically intense cross country skiing coupled with target shooting where one is so controlled they can manage a shot to bullseye between beats of their heart.) And while

I primarily give attention to physiological and cognitive readiness during competition, I speak to the rituals of readiness that increase motivation in preseason, offseason, and postseason, mindful that each of these seasons is compounded when planning an annual program with macro cycles, micro cycles and meso cycles.

When teams have equivalent talent and coaches have equivalent knowledge of the sport, the difference in the outcome may come down to the coach's success in orchestrating team motivation throughout the year to yield a symphony, which culminates in a win. If done well, the intelligent observer will say, "Wow, they make it look so easy!" and the casual observer will say, "Coach has a good team. They have the talent—if I had a team like that I would be winning, too." Superior coaches and athletes do indeed make it look easy. No one sees them practicing after everyone after everyone else has gone home or sees the coach up beyond midnight going over one more game film.

Physiological readiness and cognitive readiness for a sport are two key elements in discussing motivation. These two elements are presented here in the context of game day. Considerable research has been done on the concept of motivation in sport as associated with arousal represented as an inverted U-shaped curve.

Graph 2

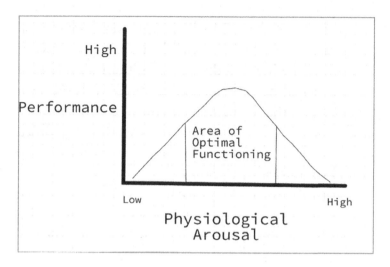

With the curve presented here (Graph 2) it is clear that with low physiological arousal, one generates low performance. This is often seen as low motivation. Reasons for low arousal can range from having an illness to relational distraction, as in, "My girlfriend broke up with me and I am not motivated to do anything today." By the way, this is a big reason why coaches isolate athletes before competition. The need to control anything that can distract from optimal motivation is important on game day.

When arousal is too high, performance also drops to a low point. Physiological stress and anxiety can certainly do this to an athlete.

Between these two extremes is the area of optimal functioning of the athlete. Opposing team coaches strategically attempt to move an athlete out of the area of over arousal by, for example, calling a time out before a competitor shoots a free throw in basketball or attempts a field goal in football.

The intention is to generate heightened arousal and with it there is increased muscle tension, which can result in either a rim shot or a kicked football veering away from the goal posts. Also, coaches will bench athletes whose arousal for the game seems low and then monitor the athlete to see if they are increasing in arousal (motivation) while sitting on the bench. As the song goes, "Put me in coach, I'm ready to play, today!" If the coach does not see this in the athlete, there is a risk the athlete can become a bench rider for the duration of the game or season.

The graph presented above dates to 1908 and was developed by Yerkes and Dodson. It is a famous theory in psychology. Other theorists have modified this, and the next graph presented is perhaps one of the clearest in terms of recognizing the value of attending to both physiological (neuro-muscular) and cognitive (frontal brain) arousal.

Graph 3

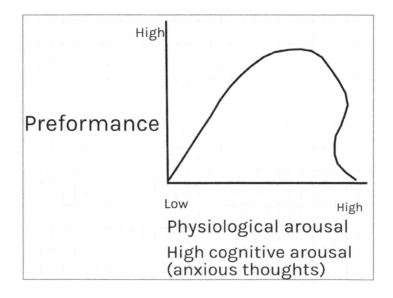

THE HUMAN DIMENSION

Here (Graph 3) the bell-shaped curve takes on a very different form. Once the addition of cognitive anxiety is added, you see a rapid drop off in performance. This can be an acute or chronic problem for the athlete.

To best understand the effect of cognitive anxiety we need to briefly consider *flow*. An athlete who, in a game, is in a state of flow is generally considered to be fully present in the moment, is in control of the situation and can execute well-learned plays with smoothness and rhythm, just as does a concert pianist who is lost in the concert and does not need to think about foot pedals or key strokes. One flows with the moment and executes the concert or the game win.

To flow, one cannot be highly anxious, as anxiety has the physiological effect of tensing muscles and the cognitive effect of producing distracting self-talk. Also, instead of the player having awareness of the whole court in front them, vision becomes tunneled and awareness of the periphery is lost.

As an example, Jake, a high school point guard in basketball, has an excellent three point shot which draws the defense close to him and that gives him the opportunity to execute his patented fall away shot or pass to an open teammate. As he goes to college he becomes very self-aware in the new environment and is prone to thoughts on the court of, "Will I make this?" As a result, he does not notice rapidly increasing muscle tension and becomes prone to tossing up air balls. This in turn cascades to disrupt the flow of the game. Now, instead of shooting his fade away or passing, which is a quick and almost intuitive decision, he actively thinks, "Should I shoot? No, not now. I will pass." The fewer shots he takes the more likely he is to miss and the more likely the opposing coach will change the defense to purely "block his pass." Flow is gone. Self-doubt emerges, and body tension is slightly higher than needed. Self-talk persists. Vision becomes tunnel so that open players are not noticed, and finally, thanks to negative self-thoughts, the athlete *self-handicaps* by saying to himself, "I was good in high school, but college is a step up and I don't have it—maybe a summer clinic..."

This example explains why the inverted U changes with increased cognitive arousal. In this instance, it is a good time to bring in a sport psychologist or related specialist to talk to you and/or your athlete. The specialist may meet with athlete and coach to provide specific strategies to return the athlete to flow, or she may need to conduct the intervention. If the athlete has a good relationship with the coach, the coach can help him self-monitor self- talk by having him write down his thoughts and feelings after the game about what happened before the shot and after the shot. This can be useful in developing such interventions as *reattribution training* and *cognitive restructuring*, combined with *in vivo* (in life) exposure with feedback that can help the athlete return to good flow over time.

A similar response would be appropriate for the athlete who plays well in season but at critical times during the big games has a low percentage of success. This is a phenomenon familiarly known in popular culture as choking. Fans have watched over and over again as a player is having a great game or season and seems destined to win when suddenly performance deteriorates resulting in a game loss, often at a critical moment in the season or postseason. Choking can happen to an individual or a team and can easily set the stage for self-doubt, self-handicapping and reinforcement of negative performance in future games.

In this case, a sport-specific intervention is very important as soon as possible. Blaming the athlete for the loss (which fans and media of course inevitably do) is the best way to set the athlete up for future failure. When the time is appropriate for coach and athlete to come together, without other teammates present, this is a good occasion to execute the ABC approach to intervention.

The ABC approach includes investigating Antecedents, Behaviors and Consequences and doing it within the context of what the person was thinking, feeling and doing. This can bring out a distinction between identifying internal factors affecting performance and external factors affecting performance.

A coach may think there is no reason to use ABC because the coach saw the behavior. However, the athlete's experience of the behavior may be quite different (recall chapter 3 where it is the athlete's experience that is very important to identify if change is to occur).

Let's look at some examples of how the ABC approach can work. A hockey player's out-of-town girlfriend comes to a game and his in-town girlfriend is there. He is aware that both are there and as he enters the third period this distraction causes him to be off by about one second, which is time enough to make considerable mistakes. While this young man's lifestyle is not recommended for many reasons, the consequences on his athletic performance turn out to be significant.

Unaware of the young man's entangled romantic enterprises, the hockey coach thinks this athlete is fatigued because he can see his timing is off in the game. Following the game, the coach asks, "What happened in the third period?" (B=behavior) to which the athlete responds, "I saw my old girlfriend in the arena and my new girlfriend is here." The antecedent (A) was the athlete looking into the crowd, so the coach asks, "Why were you looking at the crowd?" The athlete responds, "Coach, she was wearing bright red and stood right behind the goal." For C (consequence) the coach says, "Okay this has not happened to you before; speak with your friends about staying in the bleachers in the future." Coach thinks to himself, "I may need to have security block off the area behind the goal in the future."

This example of the use of the ABC model yields an easy remedy. It appears that the external stimuli that brought about the choking situation with the athlete can be resolved with a straightforward solution. The next example does not involve anyone wearing bright red, but instead is an instance of choking which occurs from internal factors to the athlete.

Aiden is a high school senior and a very competitive triple jumper. During the past meet he fouled out, yet his training has been very good. Using the ABC model, the coach sees nothing in the current environment that could have affected the timing of Aiden's jump. Indeed, athletes he usually competes against are all on their usual times with two setting personal records for themselves. Coach reviews the video and sees Aiden appears to be glancing down at the foul line where he has not done this in the past (B= behavior). Coach talks with Aiden and shows him the film of his jumps. Upon asking Aiden about his change in behavior, Aiden says, "Coach, I grew a lot this summer and my friends say that growth will throw my timing off and I am unsure…" (A= antecedent). For C (consequence) the coach discusses the fact that change has minimally occurred in his stride length and that they would increase run up trials in their practices to make adjustments as needed.

In the previous examples, the ABC model offers a great assist. The model works providing the coach addresses both what the athlete was feeling and thinking prior to the behavior and following the behavior. The failure to evaluate the behavior can result in poor habits and/or negative self-talk setting in, and that can be hard to change in the future.

Good coaches almost intuitively use techniques of cognitive restructuring and *reframing*. In the example of the triple jump athlete, the coach, after employing ABC, reframed the situation by: 1) challenging the athlete's assumptions, 2) reframing the assumption to "if you return to your previous technique with adjustment for growth you will do well" and 3) putting it into practice. Generally, these techniques address both emotions and thoughts relative to behavior.

While reframing is often used by a person on their own, cognitive restructuring is generally used as part of a therapeutic modality. It is valuable in addressing cognitive distortions. One example includes an athlete's belief that they cannot make the transition from high school to college. Another is "mind reading," whereby the athlete believes the coach does not like him or her and worries they will be pulled out of the game in favor of coach's beloved athlete. Or, the athlete believes that if they don't get a good night's sleep the night before the game they will have a poor performance and as a result they lie awake thinking about not being able to sleep.

For a coach to attempt cognitive restructuring it is important to do so in a calm environment off the field where they can identify the situation and analyze the thoughts and feelings of the athlete, especially automatic thoughts the athlete may have interfering in the game (here an athlete's journal is important). The coach then needs to find and provide support for alternative explanations the athlete may use to modify behavior. Here the support of an assistant coach and captain are very important. For instance, an athlete is not likely to tell a head coach that they believe they are not liked by coach. Also, the use of a sports psychologist as consultant to best assist the coach via instruction and feedback can be a very valuable tool. This coach-based consultation is under-utilized and has great value if applied with care and feedback.

In regards to the application of the method above, team captains can play a critical role in helping with team motivation. The best captains are not always the best players on the team. They are the people who are empathic, strong of character, have good social intelligence and work well with others. Therefore, when something happens with a team member, the team, following the captain's lead, supports the member while working with the coach. One instance comes to mind that demonstrates the value of a good captain. A freshman woman was running behind the team captain during training in hill repeats. The captain appeared to be working hard and the freshman did not appear to be struggling. Both were called over and coach asked the captain, "What would you say if one of your teammates could pass you during hill training, but is uncertain about passing a senior captain?" The captain replied, "That would not help me improve my skills and I would ask her not to do that so I can continue to work hard and be challenged." The freshman passed her on the next hill. By the way, it is important to have a good enough relationship with your captains to have a prior idea of how they will respond in such a situation.

Another practical example of managing cognitive over-arousal with athletes is a variation of systematic desensitization with *in vivo* exposure. Here, you gradually desensitize the arousal-producing event by pairing progressive increases in arousal with a relaxation response. Later this technique can be applied in life *in-vivo*.

In my experience young athletes have a difficult time with solo attempts at relaxation. However, preseason and early season yoga sessions can be used as a tool to this end. Good yoga instructors can work well with the team (many teams have no nationally certified strength and conditioning coaches). They will provide an emphasis on strength early in the season and later in the season emphasize flexibility. Clearly, this varies with team needs, and the coach needs to have a good relationship with a yoga instructor willing to work with the coach and athletes.

The end of a yoga session usually concludes with Savasana, which is a relaxed pose. Here, athletes have completed the routine and are in a relaxed posture. This can be used to memorize a cue word or behavior which helps an athlete later. A general example is an athlete preparing for an 8-kilometer race. Following general warm-ups and the adjustment of racing gear, the athlete can take a few breaths, remembering Savasana and bringing arousal to a competitive state (obviously not a fully relaxed state) and perform a brief self-check of his or her early race strategy—for example, avoiding going out too fast and dying on course. Another example is an athlete at the free throw line in basketball whose habit is to rapidly dribble five times, set and shoot. He can preface his routine by taking a breath and rolling his shoulders as a cue to feel and modulate tension, then rapidly dribble five times, set and shoot. This might be a helpful remedy for an athlete who may be dropping percentage points from their average game due to hyper-cognitive arousal.

Note, this activity includes a muscular, cognitive and behavioral component allowing for self-check. Here, a relationship with a sports psychologist for review (especially with an athlete who may be losing prior gains) would be quite valuable. You may be thinking, I cannot afford a sports psychologist, and yet there are many retired psychologists in most communities who would be happy to consult in the capacity of a knowledgeable person, not for pay or to diagnose or to do therapy, which may not be possible if they retired their license. Also, many young professionals would be happy to volunteer on occasion as it has mutual benefits. And of course, you can always be on the look-out for a mentor who may find meaning and joy in mentoring a developing coach.

I offer one final example of an intervention to improve and athlete's cognitive readiness to compete, this one specific to endurance sport activities. As a quick background, I worked in the field of chronic pain and under the mentorship of top-level health psychologists, and therefore have a strategy sheet based on a list developed by Robert Kerns, PhD, a leading specialist in Health Psychology. The sheet has been valuable in helping athletes who are attempting to manage the pain and discomfort which is part of their sport.

Our athlete is a young woman who is 3 kilometers into a 5-kilometer-high school race. She is running where there is no crowd and her brain says to her, "Keep up this pace and you will not finish the race." This, despite the fact she was well disciplined in the early part of the race and her pace is something she could objectively maintain. What was going on? The athlete's brain was pleading its case. It is fascinating that our brains seek balance and if there is discomfort or pain in the body the brain pleads to return to baseline. Most of the time this is a very adaptive function and should be respected. But here the athlete is conditioned, in good health and well trained. Yet the brain pleads, barters and conspires against her. Here are examples of strategies to overcome this intrusion:

a. *Imaginative inattention.* Ignore the intense stimulation and engage in mental imagery that is incompatible, such as, "Remember following Savasana we practiced calm and I will relax to let my body flow and drop excess tension, let shoulders and arms relax so the movement is fluid…"

b. *Focus on physical characteristics of the environment.* "I am not running to the finish line, just that turn about 300 feet ahead and at that point I may slow down" (Of course she sets her new goal at that point.) Or a game strategy of," I hurt but I will pass that athlete on the next turn and accelerate when she can't see me to get a mental edge because she hurts maybe more than me."

c. *Imaginative transformation of pain.* This is minimizing the sensations. For example, "Together my teammates and I all hurt and together we will win. This pain is really motivation to run together in spirit."

d. *Mental Distractions.* Focus attention on thoughts or images. "Tonight, I will be lying in bed thinking of how I stepped off my pace and I will regret doing it. I don't want to be in regret later..." Or, the thought of looking back after the finish line knowing I am ahead of that opponent who I have been aiming to beat.

e. *Imaginative transformation of context.* This is where the intense stimulation is different from the actual situation such as when a team is running for a person with cancer or running with joy into the Olympic stadium (even though it is the first meet of the season).

f. *Dissociation.* Focus attention on the part of the body receiving intense sensations in a dissociative manner.

g. *Denial*—Telling yourself you are not in danger and it really does not hurt very bad.

It is my experience that denial does not work as well as some of the other techniques. I knew a nationally ranked junior high runner who would tell herself to be the last to step off the start line, and then gradually pass everyone else until there was no one else to pass, and then she would make believe someone was ahead of her. She combined both 'a' and 'd' above in a manner that was successful for her. Discussing these strategies in preseason and then following up with athlete's diaries for what works for them can be a valuable resource.

The above examples involve in-game evaluation of factors affecting performance. We need now to consider pre-game, week of big game and offseason training. During pre-competition on the day of competition most all good athletes and coaches feel a sense of anxiety in readiness to perform. Being in the center of the inverted curve means you are indeed anxious but hopefully not so much that you forget to eat in preparation to perform. Some athletes will say they are calm and cool and yet they are nervously listening to their music and cognitively rehearsing their strategies again and again in their head. Coaches also feel game day arousal and apprehension. As such, it is not unusual for a good coach who came up with a solid game strategy to change that strategy on game day due to apprehension, thereby resulting in a loss. It is one thing to change a strategy because environmental conditions dictate or because a top player on the opposing team has fallen ill; it is another to respond to a feeling based on anxiety. Unless there are clear data dictating a change, don't make big changes on game day!

Game day preparation is like being a pilot on a plane. For the pilot, from the first weather check early in the morning until the pilot is cleared to take the active runway, all the pre-flight preparation is highly structured with clear organization and boundaries. There are checklists to cover and procedures to follow. It is the same for the athlete.

On game day when the athlete rises in the morning with that uncomfortable feeling that dictates, "I am not hungry and if I eat I may puke later," the day must be prescribed. We train for game day.

If the team always practice in the afternoon the body is ready for afternoon practice. If the game is a late morning game then there is a rise earlier than usual so the body feels it is later in the day. If the athlete feels anxious, a pre-meal light jog is in order. Also, long before game day, practice of relaxation via whichever technique works best for the athlete may be in order. The athlete will want to cognitively ruminate on the game, so give the athlete a limited time following eating to review in their head. Prior to that, if the athlete begins to ruminate they are to say to themselves, "No, not now, I will do this for 20 minutes after I eat." That way they set time boundaries on worrying. Scheduling depression or worry time is one of the techniques developed by Aaron Beck, MD, for working with depressed people to time-limit depression and subsequently have non depressed moments.

During preseason, it is a good idea to have seasoned athletes discuss what they prefer to eat on game day. What they prefer to eat is only voluntarily shared with each other, not required. It is amazing how many marathoners have a bagel, peanut butter and banana on marathon day. To remove the bagel on the day of the game could have the same effect as not letting a batter tap home plate with the bat before setting up to swing at the ball. Denying athletes their game and pre-game habits is inviting disaster. Therefore, any changes are best done through discussion and reason, and then as a gradual approach, not as a command or dictate.

As discussed in preseason (and groundwork must be established there), once in sight of the coach, everything is controlled. If an athlete must contact parents, coach is informed in advance. Nothing is left to chance. Except for an emergency, no texting or social media until released by the coach. All activity before the start of the game is known and familiar to the athlete. Even down time, where athletes are using the restroom or adjusting their game shoes, is structured and known.

Pre-game decisions can easily affect game outcome. For example, with cross country meets, do you want the team to set up near the start line where they can feel the excitement of the day or away from the start line where they can focus on team and mental preparation? If you have a lacrosse team playing a school they have never seen before, do you want to arrive early so they can see the venue or keep to usual game day strategy?

Overall, clear structure has a calming effect on the athletes, as does an outwardly calm coach who has the leadership appearance of being in control. Having said this, I know a state title-winning coach who is very excited on game day and the athletes clearly know she will be excited. However, it is controlled excitement to benefit the athlete and this is her usual behavior and it works. All this pre-game planning allows the athlete to remain within the healthy level of arousal in the inverted U curve.

Postseason is a very important time for the athlete to physically and mentally recover and renew. It is a time to take a break from the sport and do anything but that sport. The down side of postseason is an area that has not been well studied. Some athletes coming from high physical intensity sports find postseason a time to enjoy some dietary indiscretions that are well deserved. However, in my experience, I have heard comments similar to, "I feel like a pig because I am eating this wonderful food I don't eat in season and I am not exercising the way I normally do." Or, it is not unusual for an athlete to feel burned out on the sport, especially following a final game resulting in a loss. It is important to prepare the athlete for postseason recovery and let them know that these feelings are normal and that given time they will miss the sport or move on to another sport.

Offseason training can be challenging to the coach. For the young athlete, playing a different sport has many advantages physically and mentally. It offers structure, discipline, conditioning and the joy of competition.

For school programs, training in the summer is very challenging. Many programs do not allow coach contact in any significant form during the summer. This requires pre-planning with athletes prior to summer. A young athlete who is working as a landscaper during the summer will have low energy reserves in the evening to condition. Knowing their teammates are doing their home programs at 5pm motivates them with the realization that this is a time they can feel mentally connected. Otherwise, as noted previously, morning workouts are best for compliance. For members to have a buddy system and to check in with each other can be a great value. Captains' cookouts are fun activities for teammates to look forward to and to stay on program (no coach involved).

Because athletes are not supervised, summer programs should not be intense, so as to minimize injury prospects. Summer camps are great opportunities to have connections among athletes. Also, summer camps provide opportunities for student athletes to work, play and share with fellow campers who during the season of competition may be on the opposing team. This provides valuable life learning experiences for our youth. Indeed, on one occasion, I was recruiting at a large venue where I noticed a high school student from one team run over to another team and hug the friend she had made at summer camp.

This chapter only grazed the surface of the challenges facing coaches in areas of motivation and dealing with cognitive, behavioral and emotional challenges facing athletes. For more in-depth approaches the reader may want to read more about implementing and integrating psychological skills training. The texts *Foundations of Sport and Exercise Psychology* by Robert Weinberg and *Applied Sport Psychology* by Jean Williams are two examples where the reader can find good information on these topics.

Maximizing physiological and cognitive readiness can and often does make all the difference in a competition. Keeping athletes motivated so they reach their optimal level of performance at the right time is important to success. It requires being able to execute the ABC's in a timely and appropriate way, and like much else in this book, it requires knowing one's athletes and being attuned to the devil that might be lurking in the physiological or cognitive details of their athlete's performance.

TEN

GETTING INTO COLLEGE

The title of this chapter suggests it is a guide for athletes who want to go to college. While this is partially true, it is also/mainly a chapter for you, the coach as guide. When a high school coach has an opportunity to speak to a representative from a DI University on behalf of a star athlete and help advise that athlete towards his or her best option, that can be an exciting experience. However, the vast majority of the student athletes you coach don't have large university programs seeking their talents. They may or may not end up contributing to a competitive sports program at the collegiate level. Like the star recruited athlete, these students merit your guidance.

When I first started college level teaching I recall walking into the classroom to see well over thirty students sitting there waiting to greet their professor. I did not have to recruit them. I did not know their parents, their likes or dislikes or their motivation. Later in my career as I began coaching, my eyes were opened to an incredibly different experience.

Recognizing that I would need to recruit athletes, visit their school, their guidance counselor, their coach, observe their game performance, meet their parents, seek out their transcripts and academic performance, communicate with our college admissions office, set priorities for admission, communicate that to our athletics department and recommend admissions for some, it became clear a coach knows their athlete in a way a teacher rarely knows their student.

This became a fascinating journey full of the challenges I had not experienced as a professor. Coach/professor/ businessperson/salesperson/advocate/mentor/guide is a fascinating combination—requiring lots of delicate balance. It has also yielded a richly rewarding, if steadfastly challenging, life as a coach.

I recall the first time a college athlete whom I did not have in class asked for a graduate school recommendation. As a professor, I have recommended many students based on their academic performance, research skills and related talents. Recommending this student to a graduate program seemed a bit of a puzzle, as I had not witnessed their academic performance. I recall taking a long run and thinking, "What does this coach have to offer that could help this wonderful student athlete gain admission?"

After the run it became clear to me that the qualities possessed by this student athlete were ideally suited for graduate school. This person demonstrated discipline, organization, perseverance and character as well as excellent relational skills and a high social intelligence. Oh yes, he also had a wonderful sense of team fair play.

These are the qualities one would want when working with an analytical team in a chemistry or biology lab. The combination of the letter of reference along with a solid grade point average and letter from the faculty helped this athlete gain entrance into a top tier doctoral program.

Often, it seems the coach's role is to fit the student to an athletic program, when in fact, for most student athletes it is to fit the student to the proper academic experience and environment where they can thrive as a person *and* continue to also develop their athletic skills. I have seen athletes enter colleges who were offered good scholarships and playing time. When the athlete did not "fit" with the college (too big, too small, rural versus urban, you name it) they suffered at all levels, including sports. Further, a program may offer much to the athlete but if there is not a good fit with personality or temperament of the coach it is a recipe for disaster. The exception is the highly talented top tier student who can suffer the relationship for the benefit of the sport they love and the professional sports contract they desire. This comprises less than 1% of student athletes.

It may seem unusual for a high school coach to author a letter of recommendation for a student athlete who will not be playing sports in college. However, as noted above, highlighting strengths, challenges met and promise may be exactly what is needed to secure admission. In this capacity, the coach may be the ideal reference person.

For example, a coach may know that Jasmine came to practice each day with worn shoes and excellent spirit. Jasmine, who has four siblings and a working parent, divided her time between sports, studies, a part-time job and baby-sitting her siblings. The coach can speak to her unfulfilled academic potential as well as the strength of character and future possibilities inherent in Jasmine.

This may be especially true of the remotely-rural adolescent from a tiny school or the inner-city minority student, neither of whom have test scores or grades that reflect their full potential. For these adolescents, their coaches may be the critical link between their graduating from high school and going to college. I have known such students who have not only succeeded in college after struggling for a year or two in adapting, but also went further to receive their doctoral degree and hold very influential positions in their community. We all mature in our own way and at different times.

There are many books out there and many resources on the internet that will help the all-star athlete get into the school of his or her choice. But for the average student athlete with potential, there is you, their coach/guide.

The National Collegiate Athletic Association has developed rules that apply to all athletes applying to college. While all must comply, many of the rules were developed for the high-end athlete to assure they are not disadvantaged by coaches.

However, the average student athlete typically goes unnoticed. If a rule is broken, there are sanctions. But the average student has little clue of the myriad of rules. And yet, on occasion, it is the unknown high school student who navigates their way forward and becomes the rock star. If you doubt this, just give Michael Jordon a call.

My mentor, coach George Davis, won a National DII title in cross country while he was coaching at UMass Lowell. He won with exactly those type of individuals who became rock stars in their sport thanks to dedication, very hard work and a superior coach. We need to protect all our athletes, and as a coach/guide, you cannot underestimate your value in guiding your student athletes to their next step by helping them get into the college that is right for them.

What follows is an interview I conducted with Eric Nichols, Vice President of Enrollment Management at Loyola University. I had the pleasure of serving with Eric when he was in this role at Saint Anselm College, and I came to appreciate his grasp of the big picture as well as the particular complexities of the higher education admissions world. I think his insights are a great resource for all coaches who might play a role in guiding their student athletes towards preparing themselves for and choosing the right place to continue their education, and quite possibly their sport.

Me: You are reviewing the application of an average high school student athlete with potential. The coach at this college has a modest interest in this athlete but is not pressing for him or her to be admitted. What is it you like to see with the applicant that would help her or him gain admission to your college?

Eric: What is helpful obviously is the understanding that overall, they are admissible to the college and there is interest from the coach. We want to know that the student has put an effort into demonstrating their actual interest in the school. You can tell if they are just throwing [their application] together to get it in, either because they have to or due to the coach's interest. That can work against them if it is academically close.

Some advice coaches can help with when they are mentoring is don't let your athletes take anything for granted. The process the athlete takes with the coaching staff at the college level and the admissions process are actually separate. Just because the coach is interested in you does not mean you get into the college every time. Make sure to cover both your bases and put as much into the application showing you are interested in the college as the sport you will be playing.

Me: Let's say you have a son or daughter of modest academic and athletic ability looking to apply to a Division I or II or III. What would you advise them?

Eric: Division III has no athletic scholarship. In this division there is less emphasis on the sports and more emphasis on academics. I would say it is the same for DII as well. You can get a small scholarship, for example, in sport A, and a full scholarship in sport B. There are limits to scholarships in DII, or you may not get anything in DII. And so, when you are thinking about going to college, think of the broken leg test. If you broke your leg and couldn't play the sport anymore would you still be happy with the school you are choosing? For DII or DIII you should never be putting the sport before the school.

Even at fully funded levels you see transfers happen either because of injury, or because they don't get the playing time they thought they wanted, and they just are not happy. That can happen at the DI level as much as the others.

Also, while DII and DIII athletes get little or no athletic money, they may get full financial assistance because of other funding sources, such as need-based and merit-based awards. If a student stops playing that sport, they still get that money. Need may fluctuate based on family factors but in the case of merit you have earned it as long as you maintain the minimal grade point average at the school. You don't have to worry about losing that money.

Me: Does the average student have a better chance when applying early given colleges have admission goals?

Admissions Director: At some schools it does not make a difference when you apply—early action versus early decision. There is a higher turnover [in admissions] for early decision as it is binding. Student athletes tend to do that as they are planning on signing a national letter of intent anyway. On the admissions side, colleges have their goals of applicants they are looking for, whether it is gender, program [major], where the student is from or whether they play a sport. Sometimes applying early action helps, but since many students are applying early anyhow it does not necessarily give you an advantage

Me: If it were your son or daughter—at that age the young person changes their mind a lot—if they are not getting a big scholarship and are moderate to highly interested in a college, would you still encourage early decision?

Admissions Director: Students do change their mind. I counsel students here that if finances are a factor they probably should not apply early decision because you don't get the chance to compare financial aid packages, especially the student athlete where there is low or no scholarship involved. Sometimes it is best for the family to compare types of packages they are getting from other schools and early decision won't give them the chance to do that. So, that is a reason to think long and hard about making that decision. What a student wants when they enter their application the summer before senior year may change. We have seen students try to get out of early decision because they have had a change of heart. I always say, give yourself the most flexibility, and early action is a good combination of knowing your status and still having until May 1 to make your decision.

Me: Do many colleges have sports that the college calls flagship, where student x has a full ride for a flagship sport and another student athlete in a different sport receives much less if any money?

Eric: Yes, so especially DII schools do not have enough aid to fund to the DII limit. Some students in one sport may be getting a full ride or close to it and another not getting anything. Each school makes a decision to allocate resources a certain way. When there are large differences on the same team in athletic scholarships, that is a judgment the coaches have to make. Differences between sports is not usually [due to] the caliber of the athlete, it is the budgets. (The interviewer notes here that some coaches bundle all athletic, merit and need money to make it sound attractive, but it is only partially athletic, and the athlete may have received the money whether or not/regardless of whether they play a sport in college.)

Me: I have coached both men and women. It seems the female applicant is generally more organized earlier in the application process and men tend to delay and often apply following pressure by their parents. I have looked more carefully at the application of the young male applicant in the fall because it is less typical behavior for the male athlete. This is unless, of course, it is a DI scholarship athlete being heavily recruited.

Eric: I laugh in response to the question because it is not unique. I don't mind saying this about my own gender; girls are smarter and more organized. Also, there are more women in the country and statistically more women going to college because they just seem readier for it. If we just looked at early action, we would be about 70% female, and we end up about 60% female because the majority of our applicants who apply regular decision are men and they apply late. That is a trend across the country in all types of institutions and it is not new. It has not changed in the past ten years.

Me: Let's say a coach sends two potential athletes who are wonderful, five who are ok and you need to decide among those five. Does intended major ever make a difference?

Eric: Sometimes, and this varies by school. For student athletes on the edge academically, the major can be a factor when a major is competitive. On the flip side, sometimes at highly selective schools, if a student wants a major that is not popular it can make a difference, but in my experience, it has not typically been a difference maker. That is where the application filled out well comes into play. Evidence in the application of their involvements outside the classroom can demonstrate true interest in that major.

Me: Does it help for a parent to contact their desired college if they have a better financial offer from a less desirable college?

Admissions Director: I think it has become more the norm for parents, because college has become more expensive, to say, "This is what my daughter has been offered, is there anything this college can do financially for me." 15 years ago, it was inappropriate to do that. I think it is perfectly fine to do that now because things have changed. Colleges have become a lot more expensive. Having said that, families have to be prepared to hear the answer no, especially on the merit side, because where they fall in the admit pool for one school might be very different for another school and that is a product of the competition in that school's pool and it is not a reflection on the student. When there are differences in need analysis, there are times when it is beneficial to check with the admissions office to see if more can be done.

Me: What about when one college offers generous funding to the student in the freshman and sophomore years and then drops it off junior or senior years so there is poor consistency over 4 years?

Eric: Yes, people need to ask that question for transparency. We hear it all the time when families visit. It is called the bait and switch package. Many of the schools in our area that we compete with do not do bait and switch packages, but it is a question that you should ask when you visit campus. There is no way to determine that when going onto the websites. You have to ask, "Are there examples of grant aid I may receive as a freshman that may not follow?" Most schools are pretty good about keeping things even.

Me: How important is it for a coach to send an athlete out for an overnight at their college of interest?

Eric: I think it is pretty important. In some cases, schools don't do it for the regular population, but do it for athletes. If you can take advantage of that type of program you are a) trying to determine whether you are comfortable there in general and b) usually you are staying with potential roommates. It is a great idea and I think more athletes should do it.

Me: How important is it for a coach to direct a recommendation to a college with information indicating the coach knows the college versus a writing a generic letter?

Eric: It is helpful but when we are getting recommendations from coaches, teachers, school counselors the most important thing is that they know the student well. Can you tell us something about the student? With a letter from a coach it is usually how they worked well on the team. How did they overcome adversity? Those are the things that are important. I am less concerned that the coach knows about us. It is important that the student knows us and is interested in us. It is important that the coach tells us something new that we did not know about the applicant.

Me: So, more important than the win/loss record is the character of the person?

Eric: Correct. As much as anything else in a letter of recommendation, *it is not about accomplishments it is about setbacks.* Sometimes people writing letters are afraid to bring up anything negative, but we all know life isn't perfect. Things go wrong and students who are most successful are the ones who can bounce back. So, having an understanding that they have been through [something negative] and did well and learned something is important, and we don't see as much of that in recommendation letters as we should.

By now, it is clear, as a coach you can have a powerful effect on your athlete's life. Your recommendation can open doors for your athletes whether or not they plan to play sports in college. To follow the recommendations offered by Eric can place your athlete in their best position for college admission and a successful college career.

ELEVEN

REFLECTIONS FROM SENIOR COACHES

hile preparing to write this chapter, I was invited to give the annual dinner address to a group of athletic training staff. These professionals work at the high school level. The session went well and it was a joy to interact with a group of seasoned professionals who are committed to their student athletes. At the end of the session I asked about their relationship with coaches. These trainers all believe it is important to have a good relationship with coaches, with one trainer observing, "When you [work with] the coach you can see a decrease in injuries." The trainers believe it is okay to challenge a coach when necessary. This conversation reinforced for me once again what I have stated several times in the course of this book; namely, how important it is for the coach to know all the key players who work with the team.

When a trainer can trust a coach's judgment and the coach trust the trainer, you have part of the necessary foundation for a successful team. No coach wants to see a trainer pull an athlete from a big game for something that seems trivial, and no trainer wants to learn that a coach believed a concussion was mild, and since it was approaching the end of the season the coach did not report the concussion to the training staff. The trainers each have a strong focus on the health and welfare of the young athletes they serve. When coaches share that passion, the coach and trainer relationship is productive and rewarding for all involved. In this chapter I wanted to do just what those trainers have done: get to know coaches so that we can better help young athletes.

Here are conversations I had with six successful coaches from different sports whose experience ranges from 20 to 50 years. What they share in common is a deep caring for the person of the young athletes they coach. I asked each of them to speak about their philosophy or underlying reason that motivates their coaching, and what coaching is all about for them. In their responses they also reflect upon some of their most memorable moments of coaching, some of the more joyful and challenging things they've faced and the challenges of coaching young male and female athletes. Their words reinforce many of the lessons from the previous chapters, and add some insights I had not included. In addition to that, their reflections are just plain inspiring. I am happy to bring this book to a close by sharing with you the voices of these thoughtful guides and teachers.

GEORGE DAVIS. Coach Davis started coaching in 1964 and "retired" in 2003. He has coached middle school, high school, college and postgraduate age groups. I place "retired" in quotation marks because while George officially stepped down from the work of full-time coaching, he continues coaching on an individual and consultative basis, and retirement has not kept him from living out his belief that there is always more to learn. To me, George will always be an admired and beloved coach. As I noted earlier in this book he is my mentor. For any athlete who worked hard for him he would work even harder for the athlete. As a mentor, he has functioned in that very same manner.

In our recent conversation Coach Davis did not mention that he coached over 100 athletes to become All Americans. He did not mention that he won National DII title with a cross country team that did not have a varsity track program, a fact which strongly affects recruiting and training for cross country. He did, however, note that he had the most wins for the brightest GPA (grade point average) team at his University.

When I asked about his philosophy of coaching, George said he attempted to develop young people to their capacity as much as he could. Also, "I would never *not* coach someone who wanted to be coached. I was not smart enough to know who was best…I looked for their expectations, not mine." One principle he said he emphasized to all his athletes was, "Work as hard as you can to your capacity."

Coach Davis says he preferred to learn rather than lecture. "I listen to get better. Others who are better can boost me up." When asked about memorable moments he said they are the relationships with the athletes. "It's the whole secret. I don't remember wins and losses, scoring changes over the years."

His advice to new coaches is, "Sit down and try to organize your philosophy. A new coach tends to do what they learned under their coach and try to improve on it. This is a challenge as they were coached to their abilities and it may be different for the athletes they will coach. Also, you need to be consistent. Make rules so you can be consistent. Rules should be broad enough to fit many situations."

Davis explained to me that he does not teach negative lessons; he does not punish. If an athlete is not ready based, for example, on limited summer training, the athlete is given a modified schedule based on their current ability. He noted, "I don't ignore or humiliate. I had a two-time All American who could not train in the summer." In my experience Coach Davis gave his attention to all those seeking to learn, regardless of their level of talent. Not receiving his attention was a clear motivation to get out there and work to earn it.

Regarding preparation, Coach Davis recommended, "Look at both sides to come up with a solid plan…it's the little things that determine the win." He added, "If the athlete does not believe it, it won't work." Davis worked hard to always modify the program to not be predictable; rather, he changes it based on the needs of the athletes.

Partially teasing, I asked Coach Davis, "When did you know you were smart enough to win?" With little hesitation, he replied, "Never…I try to continue to learn and add new things for my training. Always listen to successful people." When asked if he viewed himself as coach or mentor or teacher, he replied, "I don't like the word 'coach.' Everyone has a different opinion of the word 'coaching.' If their experience was good or not good, maybe that is what that word means to the person."

Asked about coaching both men and women, he noted that he was least prepared to adjust to coaching men and women at the same time. He compared it to speaking two different languages in the same room. The female athletes, he said, wanted more explanations about what they are doing whereas male athletes want to know, "Did you do this before and was it successful?"

Two of the most valuable takeaways from my conversation with coach Davis were not about All Americans or national titles, though George is surely proud of all these athletes. First, he emphasized that the number one factor in supporting the coaching endeavor is family. "I could not have done it without the support of family." Second, in reflecting on all the people he coached at all levels over the years, he declared, "Success is about people, not wins or losses." That is an important truth for any coach to carry, and I am grateful to have been the beneficiary of such wisdom.

BARBARA HYER. Coach Hyer has 22 years of experience coaching middle school, high school and college levels. Her primary sport as a coach has been lacrosse, though she has coached field hockey and basketball. Barbara coached college lacrosse before making a transition to high school. At the college level, Barbara coached at an exclusive school which recruited athletes from strong backgrounds.

Asked to describe her philosophy of coaching, she separates it into the two arenas she has experienced, high school and college. In high school, she says, she emphasized making it fun for the athletes. Also, she sought to teach the athletes skills and game strategy to play a good game. In college, she notes, there is considerable pressure to win and prove oneself. This was especially true as she started college coaching in her early years when she was close in age to her players. She was a solo coach for her sport and had full responsibility for recruiting, coordinating practices, and all aspects of the season and offseason.

Barbara has mentored other coaches and has done so as a player on a team with other coaches where she taught game strategy. When asked about coaching differences between male and female athletes, she found the male athletes wanted to hit hard in the game and she enjoyed seeing their enthusiasm. She found college women, at this exclusive college where she coached, tended to internalize more. Coach Hyer noted this could be a product of being a top player in high school and coming to a competitive college program and being one of many good players.

For Barbara, the most enjoyable part of the job was seeing athletes have fun and seeing what worked in practice work in the game. The least enjoyable part of coaching was seeing young women at a premier college, which emphasized independence among these intelligent adolescent athletes, exert ego and opinion. While individual independence can certainly be a virtue, it can also present a considerable challenge when it comes to building team unity.

Coach Barbara's advice to young coaches is to be 100% prepared, but also be flexible. "I used to have it all set up to the minute, yet then I would change because athletes needed more time." Also, she emphasizes, "Get to know your athletes so they can trust you." One additional recommendation Barbara makes is, "After each game, ask them what they did *well*, and what can *we* can work on to be better."

JOHN TRISCIANI ("TRISH"). Coach Trish is currently the defensive line coach on a DII football team. He has coached football for 40 years and the past 11 years has coached at the college level. He also coached baseball for 23 years. His coaching experience has been with athletes with age ranges from 9 to 23. He has been a head coach and assistant coach over the years, and he has coached winning teams as well as teams that struggled in their growth.

When asked what his biggest personal accomplishment has been, Coach Trish replied, "I don't know." Then, after thinking for a moment he said, "The relationship with players. I have gotten more from them…than I have given." That may be true, but like many coaches John is likely unaware of the enormous impact he has had on the athletes in his care.

Because I have taught and coached in the same community as Trish, I can offer an example. Once when my wife and I were dining out a server saw my college jacket and asked if I knew Trish. I said I did and the server remarked, "He saved my life in high school. I was heading down the wrong path and Coach Trish saved me." An example like this reinforces why, as I have noted in earlier chapters, I have as a psychologist written into a student's IEP that they need to continue to play their sport. Being under the guidance of people like John Trisciani may make all the difference.

College athletes who are coached by Trish have high praise for him. As the 2020 pandemic cancelled classes coaches were left to either calling or Zooming with athletes. Trish would call and Zoom with his athletes. His primary emphasis was how the student athlete was emotionally managing during the pandemic. He knew he would get to football tactics and strategy, but he needed to know the well-being of his athletes was being cared for during these challenging times.

Regarding a philosophy, Trish says, "The number 1 responsibility is to teach football and develop relationships with the players." Trish finds respect and loyalty to be very important and states that a coach cannot demand respect and loyalty; it must be earned. He notes that it's important to have a good time, to teach well and to pull strings to get the most out of the athletes. "I listen to the guys," he says.

Regarding the joys and challenges, Trish offers an enviable response that may encourage most of us; he says, "I like all of it!" He particularly enjoys, he says, the relationships he has made with colleagues who coach at all age levels of the sport. His advice to young coaches is, "Coach within your personality," and, "Be able to acknowledge when you screw up and of course, make corrections."

KELLY FOX. Coach Fox has been coaching since 2003. During these 17 years she has coached both middle school and high school cross country and track and field. She also has coached college varsity cross country. Further, she has coached both male and female teams. Coach Fox's teams have won state titles and she has a history of putting forth quality teams and getting athletes into college programs.

Coach Kelly describes her coaching philosophy this way: "In high school, I want the athletes to enjoy the sport as something they can use as a tool in life after graduation. Few athletes compete in sports in college, but they will continue in life. It is not often in a coach's career that you work with someone who will be elite, so decide as a coach, 'Do you want a strong program?' And more important, 'Do you want better runners? Better human beings and more confident people?'" Coach Fox remembers with joy having a team that lost by one point in a season and came back the following season to win the championship. She clearly indicated the win was due to her athletes' hard work and commitment. She adds that each of her teams over the years holds special memories for her.

Kelly enjoys interactions with her athletes and says she least enjoys the paperwork. Her advice to new coaches is, for cross country, there are many good books and at the high school level, "If you put forth effort and care about the kids, you won't be wrong…help them do something every day." Also, "You have to be invested in learning and working at it and care about the kids." Kelly believes it is important to always be willing to learn more, adding, "It is not wrong to feel bad…the coach takes the loss when the team does what you have asked [and loses]." Also, "For every mistake made, you need a reason or a tool."

Kelly continues, "When the big day comes, you have to watch hard…there is so much pressure on the athlete." I have seen Kelly on days of competition. She transforms from the thoughtful, even-paced and considered coach to a whirlwind of positive energy and enthusiasm while maintaining focus and clarity of thought to assist the athletes. This has a positive benefit of helping the athlete manage their pressure in competition.

When I asked Kelly if there was a question I had not asked, she replied, "How will you know when your time as a coach is done?" She believes that if a coach cannot turn a team around in 5 years it is time to consider alternatives. Kelly also added that family is very important for her. She shifted her coaching to a school closer to home so she could spend more time with her family. It is also clear to me that Kelly considers her athletes extended family. She mentors former athletes and enjoys when former athletes contact her for a hello or coaching advice. I consider myself very fortunate to coached alongside my friend and colleague Kelly Fox.

MIKE HYER. Coach Hyer was a Hall of Fame college athlete and coach who has coached high school and college lacrosse. In addition, he has also coached basketball and cross country. He has been an active coach since 1977 at the college and university levels at both mixed gender schools and at an all-women's college. In addition to these 43 years of coaching, he taught college Physical Education. His recent coaching is at the high school level.

Asked about his philosophy, he says, "Have fun. If the players understand the 'what' and 'why' of what we are trying to do, it leads to good outcomes." Mike's advice to a new coach is be prepared and be flexible. "Plan out your program but know you have to be flexible to change according to the athletes' needs." Mike added, "Know your players. I have had deep conversations with players on life and challenges. You become an important figure to athletes; be open to realize you have an impact on their lives." Mike added that during an athlete's 4 years of college, the one person they have the most contact with is their coach. Clearly, Mike sees the role of guide/mentor of the coach to the athlete as an important relationship for the developing person.

He describes what he enjoys about coaching as seeing an athlete get recognition for their work. He also enjoys building a foundation in the sport for the athlete. He observes, "Each year the coach says something similar and yet it is different." When asked about an aspect of coaching he found least enjoyable, he mentioned that for high school, building a team was hard work, but it was motivating athletes that was the challenging part of coaching. For college, recruiting was not fun, especially recruiting high end students for a prestigious women's college.

Regarding coaching men and women, Mike says that the men are more self-serving and have the attitude they will run through a wall to compete. In general, he says, if guys lose, they do not see it as their fault. For the female athlete, he says it's not uncommon that if they lose, they don't feel good, and if they win, they feel lucky. It is harder, he says, for the female athlete to take credit for the win. As such, they need more encouragement.

One final note, Mike says he went to college to be a business major. During his first semester he played in a roller derby group and found he loved coaching and that he did not have that same passion for business. Coach Hyer was drawn to coaching because he was motivated to help people understand sports and to be better athletes. Later in his coaching career, he became more appreciative of the value of helping his athletes become better people.

KERSTIN MATTHEWS. Coach Matthews has coached women's hockey for 20 years, the past 12 of those being in her current college position where her team has won 5 postseason tournaments and has been a runner up 4 times. In addition to her other accomplishments, Kerstin has successfully transitioned her team from Division II into a competitive Division I team. She is a winning coach who does not speak about her own successes.

When asked about her philosophy, Kerstin says, "The number one reason I coach is to inspire the athletes to be more confident people when they leave." She prioritizes their work as: first, academics; second, sports; and third, community involvement. Kerstin sees all three as important to the life of the student athlete.

Kerstin sees herself as a mentor to other coaches and enjoys the opportunity to mentor. When asked about gender differences in sports, she said she knows there are technical differences but tries not to distinguish. She sees her work as working with the individual athlete.

Her most enjoyable part of coaching is "seeing the athlete become comfortable in their own skin." She describes the most difficult part of the job as making cuts from the team. Also, she describes the challenge when an athlete makes bad decisions and struggles to understand why it was a bad decision.

Her advice to a new coach is to take the time to write down your philosophy as a coach. When asked what she would do if an athlete did not have the summer training needed for her program, she answered, "I would modify the program."

Coach Matthews adds that, as a coach, one needs balance in their own life. "There are times when you work on different areas of your life." While the athlete is a priority, it is clear for Coach Matthews, the coach's life must also be in balance.

FINISH LINE. Looking back on my conversations with these six remarkable coaches, I note that not once during any of the conversations did I hear the phrase, "When I won…" or even "when we won…" What they emphasized over and over was the relationship with the athletes. Each finds different aspects of their work challenging; each has various approaches to building a competitive team. Each of them is successful because in their role as a guide in developing their athletes, they are intent upon helping develop the whole person, not just the lacrosse or hockey or football or distance runner who can help with a win. In caring for the young men and women in their charge, they enhance the probability of a win.

EPILOGUE

Some years ago, a colleague of mine had an athlete competing at nationals. During a break in the competition, this colleague was listening to a fellow coach complain that his team did poorly because he only had three full scholarships. When that coach asked my colleague how many scholarships he had, my colleague replied, "We don't have scholarships." The other coach's shocked reaction, while it may sound like a put-down, was actually a form of great praise: "No scholarships? What the hell are you doing here?" His meaning in this question that was not merely rhetorical was, "Without scholarships how could you possibly have risen to this level?"

Who is the most successful coach? The coach whose athletes won at nationals that year or the coach who managed to have an athlete competing there who had not been lured or supported by a scholarship and who had a fraction of the resources to work with as the elite programs represented there? How, in other words, do we measure the success of a coach when programs and circumstances vary so widely?

Glamour University has enviable state-of-the-art facilities, plentiful support staff, a recruiting budget, scholarship money and a recognizable brand that enables them to draw athletes from around the world. Podunk State has a meager budget and one volunteer assistant coach who is one of the coach's former athletes. The program offers no scholarships and all recruiting has to be done via phone, email, or on trips whose range is limited to the capacities of the coach's old VW wagon. Who is going to have more success?

Notwithstanding the wide-ranging disparities between programs, the differences in age groups, academic vs. community-based teams and so on, I hope what is clear in what I have written in the preceding chapters is that there are some indelible traits that characterize the successful coach, whether the coach is the person guiding athletes at an elite DI university, or the parent called upon to try to salvage a small town's fledgling recreational league.

The successful coach is a student of the sport over all seasons of training and competition. This coach is highly competitive in planning strategy and tactics that are based upon his or her knowledge of the competition as well as the strengths and limitations of the current athletes. This coach seeks the best science behind trends and does not use his or her athletes to prove that a trend in sports is accurate. Rather, the successful coach attempts to ask the next question of, "What else may explain this trend?" As a student of science, this coach is a student of human behavior and relationships. Also, this coach has developed the ability to notice slight shifts in gait of the athlete, or explosive speed or ballistic blocking. This coach is able to notice from careful observation if something is off with the athlete, and careful in discerning whether the cause is neuro-muscular, cognitive understanding or emotional.

The successful coach is a teacher who knows there are many learning styles and who works hard to find the style best fitting individual athletes and the team. Additionally, this coach seeks to understand the athlete's interpretation and experiences of their world based on the athlete's sense of self-awareness and self-understanding.

On the college level and even in secondary education, it can be quite unusual to see a coach having lunch with faculty. This is unfortunate as together, both have so much to offer their student athletes. A faculty member who fashions himself or herself as purely a spokesperson of their discipline and views the students as a repository of their knowledge knows little about teaching. The successful faculty and successful coach both have keen insight and knowledge of their students and student athletes which can help motivate them to achieve their best on the page and on the field or court. Increased cross-departmental communication would advantage the student and engender some wonderful relationships.

The time has also come for primary and secondary teachers who also have coaching responsibilities to be afforded the opportunity to receive continuing education credit units for their work as coaches. Such continuing education units would be provided for courses on the human dimension of the student athlete, not the elements of their particular sport.

The successful coach has had to master a wide variety of tasks, many of which offer little satisfaction or recognition: managing a budget, raising funds, overseeing recruiting efforts, maintaining contact with alumni athletes, mentoring coaches with less experience, and interacting with parents, teachers, school nurses, trainers and bus drivers. And of course, if no such luxury is afforded, the successful coach might find him or herself putting on a bus driver's hat as well. All of these responsibilities are juggled even while caring for an athlete who is grieving a family member's death, which the athlete disclosed when the coach (probably still frustrated about a budget or transportation issue) inquired gruffly about their apparent disinterest on that particular day.

The successful coach manages all of this, even while he or she understands that they need to be the captain of their own ship. They need to manage their own emotions when others come to tell them how to best do their job or when another coach has their athlete take a cheap shot at one of her or his athletes. This coach lets the team see their passion in the sport and competition in motivating and supporting their athletes, but at the same time has control of their passion when its expression will only be destructive. Thus, their expression of passion is authentic as well as strategic.

The successful coach is a highly intelligent, socially skilled individual who can be a great resource to their community, even though their role as a knowledgeable resource is often underutilized or disregarded. For example, as a psychologist performing an evaluation of a student in need of an educational plan, it was common to have the teachers and parents complete a behavior rating scale as one component of the evaluation. However, we did not ask coaches for their input even though coaches see students in a different and active context and typically have keen insight into their behaviors.

The successful coach is one who looks back at the "job description" above and feels daunted and humbled. Recognizing their own limitations and necessary areas of growth, a coach displays empathy for the struggles of athletes who are being asked to improve their own physical, mental and emotional agility in order to compete more successfully, even while managing the many and various aspects of their own young lives. A successful coach and a successful athlete are, like any successful person, a work in progress, with this important difference: the coach is the leader, the guide, the one with the experience who has been there before, who sees the big picture and has the long view, as well as the particular challenge at a given moment.

At the end of the day, the successful coach understands and appreciates that in taking on the responsibility of coaching, he or she is coaching a young person to develop skills as an athlete, and is also helping that athlete to develop as a thriving member of their community. These goals are entirely complementary. As I said at the outset, all of us love to win championships. All of us want to develop consistently winning teams. The very best way to achieve this as a coach is to understand the people you are coaching.

I offer here one final example. When I first started coaching cross country, we had a very small team, so I always had my eyes open for potential athletes. I had seen a student running on campus who had a wonderful kinesiology of movement and who appeared tireless. As it turned out he was a runner, swimmer and bike rider who exercised daily. Exercise was most important to him and he loved to exercise. It didn't take too much work to persuade him to join our team. He agreed to run and was well prepared for the season.

He did well as the season progressed, but as we approached the date of the championship meet he became injured. He promptly had an MRI and was told if he competed he would require an extended recovery and likely be unable to exercise for about eight weeks. I told this 20-year-old it was his decision to run or not run in the championship meet, and that his decision would be respected. It was his senior year and it would be his last race. He decided to be with the team but not compete.

At the hotel the night before the meet the captains asked if they could talk with this team member as, without him, the team would not score and they could not beat their rival. I gave permission, but strongly admonished them they were allowed to speak with him, but not pressure him.

On meet day he came out with the team as was expected. What was not expected was that he took off his jacket and commenced to do strides with the team. I stopped him and seeing a crumpled-up race number pinned to his chest asked, "Sir, what are you doing?" to which he replied, "Coach, my team needs me. Without me the team cannot score."

On that day he ran injured. I was overwhelmed with pride in this athlete who ran his worst time ever that day. For on that day, this solo runner discovered something quite important. He found a team, a brotherhood, for whom he was willing to sacrifice himself and his love of exercise by significantly delaying his recovery from injury. In doing so, he discovered within himself an increased value of sacrifice for others. As it turned out the price he paid was only two weeks of recovery instead of the more grim prognosis, but he made his choice willing to sacrifice a great deal for his team, and that lesson has endured far longer than two or eight weeks.

Years later, as these alumni gathered at our lake house in preparation for an upcoming major triathlon, we reminisced about that race day. Not a word was spoken of whether we overcame our rivals that day. Instead they reminisced about their brotherhood, their shared experiences and plans for their upcoming triathlon.

These young people went on to finish their triathlon and are now separated from each other by distance, time and family obligations. What remains with them is the shared discipline, character, friendships and capacity for self-sacrifice for their beliefs and values, and for the sake of others. The wins? They matter. But in the end, the successful coach is one who has positively guided and indelibly influenced the lives of athletes as people; people, who because of the lessons they learned in great triumphs, bitter disappointments, and moments of personal and shared sacrifice, now journey through their lives with more clarity, more strength, and ultimately more happiness—and a greater capacity and willingness to guide others. Now, that is a win.

Made in the USA
Las Vegas, NV
28 January 2021